THE GOSPEL OF MARK
in its original social context

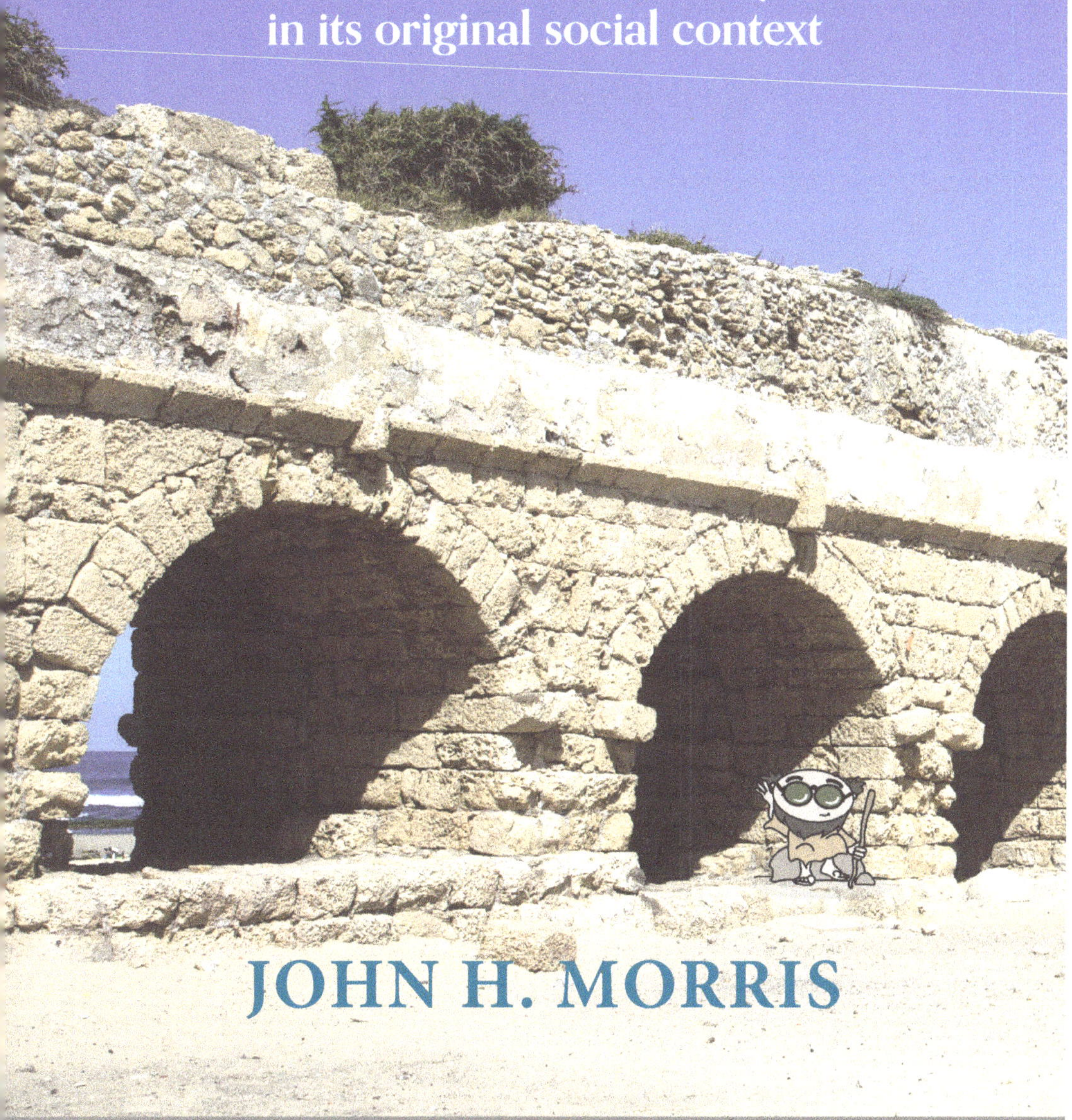

JOHN H. MORRIS

THE GOSPEL OF MARK
In Its Original Social Context

JOHN H. MORRIS

Published by JEM Publishing
in partnership with houseBLEND Publishing,
a division of PLEASANTLY DISRUPTIVE
Atlanta, GA
Copyright © 2015 John H. Morris
Photography by John H. Morris, © 2015

www.BlindBartMinistries.com

ISBN 13: 978-0-9816582-9-2
ISBN 10: 0-9816582-9-6
Printed in the United States of America

ALL RIGHTS RESERVED

Neither this book nor any part may be reproduced or transmitted in any form or by any means, electronic or mechanical, including photocopying, microfilming, and recording, or by any information storage and retrieval system, without permission in writing from the author.

For information:

JEM Publishing
Atlanta, GA
www.BlindBartMinistries.com

Table of Contents

PREFACE v

INTRODUCTION ix
          Activities: Questions for further reflection. xvii

THE GOSPEL OF MARK

Mark 1 – The Beginning of the Gospel 1
          The miracles begin 4
          Conflict and power themes 9
          Activities: Questions for further reflection. 10

Mark 2 – The Beginning of the Conflict 15
          The conflict deepens 16
          New wine and old wineskins 16
          The conflict turns deadly. 17
          Activities: Questions for further reflection. 18

Mark 3 – The Real Family of Jesus 23
          Jesus picks His disciples to be with Him 24
          Jesus' family tries a forceful intervention. 25
          The unpardonable sin 26
          Activities: Questions for further reflection. 27

Mark 4 – Jesus Teaches in Parables 31
          Devotion – The parable of the four soils 32
          Devotion – In waters just like these. 34
          Activities: Questions for further reflection. 38

**Mark 5 – The Question Answered – Who Is This
That Even The Wind and Sea Obey Him?**. 43
          Gerasene Demoniac 43
          Activities: Questions for further reflection. 46

Mark 6 – The Conflict Returns 49
          Jesus feeds the people in the wilderness 53
          Activities: Questions for further reflection. 56

Table of Contents

Mark 7 – The Conflict with the Pharisees 59
    Conflict with tradition 59
    What really defiles a person 60
    Jesus and the Syrophoenician woman 61
    Activities: Questions for further reflection. 62

Mark 8 – Jesus Teaching How to Be a Disciple 65
    Feeding the Gentiles in the wilderness 65
    Who is Jesus and what does it mean to be His disciple? 66
    Peter's Confession of Christ 68
    Activities: Questions for further reflection. 74

Mark 9 – Jesus Teaching About God's Kingdom 79
    You will see the Kingdom of God coming in power 80
    Transfiguration 80
    Disciples argue about what they saw 80
    The disciples have a "return to earth" experience 81
    Jesus predicts His death a second time
            and teaches about discipleship. 82
    Jesus uses exaggeration for effect 82
    Devotion – The power of one 85
    Activities: Questions for further reflection. 88

Mark 10 – Jesus Teaches Again on How to Be a Disciple. 93
    How do you enter the kingdom of God? 94
    Teaching about discipleship on the road to Jerusalem 95
    The healing of blind Bartimaeus 98
    The path of true discipleship is the road to Jerusalem
            and the way of the cross 98
    Activities: Questions for further reflection. 103

Mark 11– Jesus Enters Jerusalem 107
    Pictures of Jerusalem and the Temple 107
    The conquering King enters town on a donkey 109
    Parable of the fig tree and cleansing the Temple. 110
    Mountain-moving faith 112
    Let the confrontation begin 113
    Activities: Questions for further reflection. 114

Mark 12 – Jesus Indicts the Temple Leadership. 119
    Herodians and Pharisees take their best shot 120
    The Sadducees try to rally the retreating troops. 121
    A scribe finally asks a good question and gets a proper answer . . 122
    Activities: Questions for further reflection. 123

Mark 13 – The Pause Before the Passion – The "Little Apocalypse" 127
    Warning about the interpretation of Mark 13 127
    Context of the passage 127
    Grammar of the passage 128
    Abomination of Desolation 129
    The Apocalypse (end of the world) 130
    Final summary 131
    Activities: Questions for further reflection. 132

Mark 14 – The Passion Approaches 135
    The anointing of Jesus 135
    Passover 136
    Garden of Gethsemane. 137
    Devotion – Our Passover Lamb and the Kidron Valley 137
    The trial of Jesus 141
    Peter's denial of Jesus. 144
    Activities: Questions for further reflection. 145

Mark 15 – The Earthly Humiliation and Heavenly Glorification of Jesus 149
    The events 149
    Trial before Pilate. 150
    Jesus' last words on the cross 150
    God's first response to Jesus' sacrifice – the Temple veil 153
    Activities: Questions for further reflection. 154

CONCLUSION 155

Preface

Having read so many Bible commentaries in my study, I always ask myself, "Does the world need another commentary on Mark?" My normal answer is, "No," so I hope this book won't be just another commentary on Mark. This book should "fill in the corners" that a commentary doesn't get the chance to address. Many of these corners are filled with reflections about how Mark's Gospel message concerning Jesus applies to us today. This book is full of questions that I hope will prompt you to examine yourself, listen to God and decide to take some steps to become more Godly in your daily life.

My primary focus is on the actual text of Mark and what it says about Jesus. So many of us have heard the stories taught or preached so many times that we don't really hear exactly what the Biblical text says any more. For instance, have you ever **noticed** that Mark started his Gospel with three personal recommendations for Jesus? Go look and see how Mk 1 used an Old Testament prophet (Isaiah), a New Testament prophet (John) and God Himself to give references about Jesus. If you were going to introduce Jesus to someone who didn't know Him, would you want to use some impressive references? Remember that Mark didn't have Facebook or LinkedIn to show how important Jesus was. Considering that Mark wanted to emphasize Jesus' importance, he picked some pretty good references.

Normally, we hear the story of the Gerasene demoniac preached in isolation and we might wonder what the story really meant for Mark. Why was the story so important to Mark? I think the answer lies in the text itself. If we **notice** that Mk 4 ends with a question about who Jesus is, it makes sense that Mk 5 would answer that question. Now the question becomes what does Mk 5 teach us about Jesus? How has Mark used the story to reveal Jesus' character and what does the story tell us about God's kingdom?

One of the things I missed in most commentaries about Mark was an understanding of how the culture of the first century and the geography of Israel had an impact on the interpretation of the New Testament. As I discuss in the introduction, something as simple as the word "Gospel" started out as a secular Roman term with a usage different from what Christians meant by the term. The fact that Mark used it at the beginning of his Gospel message had profound Roman political implications for his Greek speaking audience.

Something as simple as the Bible noting that people always went "up" to Jerusalem and came "down from" Jerusalem continually confused me. Once I traveled to Israel, I discovered that Jerusalem, at 3000+ feet above sea level, was indeed the highest point around and that you did have to always travel "up" to get there. Furthermore, Jerusalem is built on the top of a hill, so even once you are there; you have to go "up" to Jerusalem.[1]

Jesus' charge against the Pharisees as being "white washed tombs" made perfect sense when I saw that Jesus' view from where He was teaching included a mountain hillside covered with the whitewashed tombs of people who wanted to be buried close to Jerusalem. The metaphor was clear and direct. The Pharisees were like those tombs – white and pure on the outside, but filled with corruption on the inside.

One of the things I dislike about most commentaries is their dry and academic tone. I read Mark's Gospel as living, direct and applying to me today. For that reason, I write about it in very personal terms using my normal speaking "voice." I take the Gospel personally and I hope that you will too. As a reader, please don't mistake my casual tone and occasional asides for not being serious about the Bible. I have devoted my life to studying and teaching the Bible, but I don't think that means I always have to be deadly serious about it. I have fun with what I do and that comes out in the way I communicate.

While this book can certainly be read on its own, I think it works best in conjunction with a good academic commentary and some kind of reading community. Many of the lessons you as the reader might learn require thought and discussion. The best place for this to happen is in some kind of small group. The group might be a Sunday morning class, a Bible study, a formal classroom or even an interactive on-line class. I have included a section of questions for further reflection or research at the end of each chapter, but there are many more questions raised in the

---

[1] *See the pictures on pages 137-138 for a view of Jerusalem from the bottom on the Kidron Valley.*

text than are listed. Feel free to pull anything from the text and use it as an opportunity for discussion.

I approach Mark with years of study and even more humility. Even though I work hard to read, learn from other scholars, pray and decide what I think is the truth about Mark, you have to remember that much of what is included in this book is my opinion and may be wrong. I pray that what you read is correct, but I may be wrong.

One of the best Bible scholars today, N.T. Wright, put my dilemma in perspective. I heard that he once told his class that even though he tried to be as accurate and truthful as possible, he was wrong about 20% of the time. The real problem was that he didn't know which 20% was wrong. He encouraged his class to study on their own and come to their own conclusions. I am not as good a Bible scholar as N.T. Wright; so don't be afraid to question what I have written.

On the other hand, if you read something new about Mark or see things from a different perspective than normal, don't automatically reject what I have to say. See if my thoughts fit the context and culture of Mark, don't contradict what you see in the rest of the Bible and help explain what Mark was trying to communicate. Remember, learning new things can be uncomfortable and a little bit scary. Fortunately, we have the Holy Spirit to guide us through the process.

Finally, I have done my best not to interrupt the discussion with a lot of footnotes. I understand that from an academic point of view, this is not the best practice, but I am more concerned with keeping the discussion within the Gospel of Mark and not in the many outside sources written about the Gospel of Mark.

It is customary for authors to thank their spouses for giving them time away from the family to produce whatever it is that they are writing. I am happy to say that this book didn't take time away from my wife Emma because she participated in every aspect of the work: from idea, to content creation and even to proofing. Without her not only would this book not exist, but I would be much less advanced in my Christian growth. She deserves to be a co-author of the book, but has rejected my idea to add her name. I disagree with her, but honor her desire.

Introduction

Shalom Y'all (Peace Y'all),

That may sound strange, but that could have been exactly how Jesus greeted His disciples. In the language of the New Testament, "y'all" was perfectly acceptable and part of normal usage. Even though we don't translate it that way today, Jesus used the plural form of you constantly. God's Shalom, or peace and rest, is why He came to earth for us. In that tradition, I welcome y'all aboard and pray that you will be enlightened and transformed by your experience with Mark's Gospel.

Return your seatbacks and tray tables to their normal and upright positions. Fasten your seatbelts for immediate takeoff. Put your head between your knees and assume the crash position – sorry, I got carried away there. Here we go on a devotional study in Mark. Hopefully, this book will allow you to keep things in context while we work through Mark's Gospel. I pray that we don't crash and burn and that we will exit Mark with a better understanding of who Jesus is, why we need to know about Him, and how our lives should change based on that knowledge. This book will combine teaching material on Mark with devotional questions about the application of what you are learning and should be used in addition to your textbooks and Bible reading. Hopefully, the commentary will address things that other material doesn't cover and will cause you to ask yourself questions of the Biblical text.

If you are using this book in the context of a class or small group, any question raised is fair game for discussion. As you go through, you will **notice** that I highlighted some questions or issues with a bold or italic font. The italic font indicates topics or questions that should be particularly valuable to discuss. The bold font emphasizes something in particular that I want you to **notice**. I included a list of discussion or reflection questions at the end of each chapter, but you should feel free to raise any additional issues you are interested in or you feel prompted by the Holy Spirit to include. Feel free to approach this material academically or devotionally. My prayer is that you will do both.[2]

My intent is to spend a lot of time looking at what the text says and what it meant to its original audience in their own cultural context. Once we decide that, we can ask ourselves what the text means to us and how it should be applied to our own situations today. To get started, read Mark all the way through in one sitting. In the following paragraphs, I will give you some hints about what to **notice**. Reading Mark in one session will take some time, but you need to encounter his Gospel at least once in the way that his original readers experienced it. This will also give you an overall idea what Mark's main points about Jesus are. After all, you wouldn't watch just one part of a good movie would you?

When Mark wrote his Gospel, he wrote one Gospel without any starts, stops or divisions, so don't pay much attention to the manmade chapter and verse markings. Let the story itself show you when one topic or event stops and another starts. For whatever reason, Mark only had 16 chapters to tell his audience everything they needed to know about Jesus. Because of his limited space, he must have had to make hard decisions about what to include and what to leave out. Pay attention to what Mark actually wrote and the sequence he used in his Gospel. I am convinced that all of those things are important.

Approach Mark like it was a story that you have never read. Ask yourself these questions. *Who does Mark say that Jesus is? Why do I care about this Jesus? What does this story say about Jesus? What does it say about God? What does it say about our relationship to God and Jesus?*

Don't get me wrong. When I say story, I do not doubt the absolute truth and validity of Mark's Gospel. I am not calling Mark a fairy tale, but I think one way to approach Mark with a new perspective is to look at Mark as if it were a written narrative or story. Narrative stories have characters, plots, conflicts and important endings. **Notice** how Mark uses all these narrative devices to tell his audience what they needed to know about Jesus. After all, that is why he wrote his Gospel, isn't it?

---

[2] *I have been blessed with great teachers over the years and I would like to give credit to Dr. William Warren, Dr. Gerald Stevens and Dr. Don Aderhold for sharing so much of their knowledge about Mark with me. Gilla Treibich, our good friend and tour guide from Israel, is responsible for the insight into how the geography and culture of first century Israel has an impact on our understanding of Mark Their names won't show up in the footnotes, but they are responsible for much of the wisdom in this study. I am standing on their shoulders as I create this work. The good stuff in this work belongs to them. The mistakes are all mine.*

Notice and pay particular attention to the names given to the characters and try to determine what those names tell us about the characters. I will give you a hint that names and titles are incredibly important for Mark. Much of the meaning of his story is carried in the names and titles given to people. Names conveyed power, identity and status. Allowing someone to assign a positive or negative title to you meant that you assumed the honor or status and the responsibility of living up to the positive title or acknowledging the shame of the negative title. For instance, allowing a crowd to name you as demon possessed meant that you were agreeing to accept the shame, isolation and punishment that went along with that title. You might **notice** in Mk 12:13-27 that Jesus' enemies used the title of "Teacher" as a way to trap Him. If Jesus accepted the title and the status that went along with the title and His enemies asked Him a question He couldn't answer, then Jesus would be shamed and would lose status. In turn, if Jesus asked His attackers a question they couldn't answer, they would be shamed and Jesus would gain status. **Notice** who won and lost in the exchange.

In the first century (and even today) if you didn't fight to preserve your honor and status based on your good "name," people assumed that any negative attacks must be accurate and that you deserved the shame associated with the attacks. Think about politics today. Often the truth doesn't really matter. It all depends on who can "spin" the best. If you let your opponents' negative attack messages go unanswered, everyone assumes that they must be true.

We all know that first impressions are very important, but have you ever thought about how the beginning of a story is designed to create a specific impression? Have you ever thought about why Mark started his Gospel the way he did? **Notice** what he does to catch the audience's attention and start to make his points about who Jesus is. Mark starts out his story by saying that he is writing a Gospel. Some credit him for creating the entire genre of "Gospel." One way to define a Gospel is to say that it is a narrative story about the life and meaning of Jesus. Since Mark's "Gospel" is a story, we can analyze it as a story. We have to be careful not to read 20th century concepts back into a first century document, but the narrative approach can give us fresh insights into Mark.

Before the name Gospel had a Christian meaning, it had a secular usage. When Caesar (god) won an important victory to keep his kingdom safe or had a son to secure the royal succession, he would hire "evangelists" to go out into his empire and spread the "gospel" or good news about the event. This good news would become the same word Christians used, just with a slightly different meaning. Christians took this and corrected the world's mistake about who "God" really was. The Christian Gospel said that God (not Caesar) had sent His Son to announce His kingdom. Can you image how mad Caesar was when he heard about the Gospel of Jesus Christ and His kingdom? If Mark wrote to an audience in Rome like many think, he started his Gospel with a political as well as religious bang! Of course, the kingdom Jesus preached was different from Caesar's empire, but Caesar probably didn't understand that.

We can ask certain questions about the narrative. *What is the plot? Who are the characters? What kind of conflicts do they have with each other and Jesus? What is the theme of Mark's Gospel? Why did Mark include the pieces of information that he included and why did he put them in the order that he put them in? (Most everyone agrees that Mark had more material than he used and that Mark did not arrange each piece of his Gospel in exactly the same order as they happened in Jesus' life.) Can looking at the sequence of events Mark uses in his Gospel help us interpret his meaning? How does Mark's use of characters, plot and conflict tell us about the person, nature and work of Jesus? Do the characters stay the same or do they develop during the course of the Gospel? Does this development tell us anything about Jesus and the power of the Gospel in our lives? Think how Peter changed from the trial of Jesus to just a couple of months later standing up to the religious leaders who killed Jesus. Was Peter changed by the Gospel, a view of the resurrected Christ and the inspiration of the Holy Spirit?*

As we look at individual passages, always **notice** what comes directly before and directly after the passage in question. As you will read in the story about the Gerasene demoniac, a passage's overall context will help you correctly understand the passage's meaning. So many questions and we haven't even gotten started yet. They are important questions because the answers will help us understand what Mark wanted to convey in his Gospel.

Feel free to make notes about what you **notice** as you read through Mark. After reading Mark, see if you can figure out why Mark wrote the book the way he did. *If you had 16 chapters to tell a particular group everything they needed to know about the life and purpose of Jesus, how would you do it? How would you begin and end? Remember that your beginning sets the stage in the readers' minds for the entire story and your ending will be the last thing in their minds. What are you going to do with your one chance to create a first impression?*

Would your story be based on taking everything you knew about Jesus and applying that to the needs of your audience? Is this what Mark did? Does this approach of addressing an audience's needs help us understand why the four Gospels are similar but different? What do you think Mark's main message is? Who do you think he wrote to? (Hint – **notice** *what he* *translates from Hebrew and how he explains Jewish customs. Would a Jewish audience need him to do that?) What do you think the book meant to its original readers? What does it mean to us today?*

Notice what the reader knows that the characters in the Gospel don't know. For instance, as far as we can tell by reading the Gospel, the disciples never know about the baptism of Jesus and His anointing with the Holy Spirit. The disciples don't see anything like that until the Transfiguration. *How does this affect our understanding of their actions and what does it tell us about our actions today? We have a tendency to look down on the disciples and can't understand why they can't get the message of Jesus. After all, didn't they follow him around for three years? How could they not understand what it meant to be the Son of Man and the Messiah?*

If we are careful and thoughtful readers, we will start asking ourselves if we are similar to the disciples. How long have we followed Jesus and still aren't leading the life He wants us to lead? Can we afford to look down on the disciples while we are acting as badly and misinformed as they did?

The other side of the coin is that we can be encouraged in our personal weakness and failure because Jesus never stopped loving His disciples. They worked through their problems and became faithful followers of Jesus. If an impetuous person like Peter can become a "rock" of the church, there is hope for me. As modern readers, we have to remember that Mark's original audience was reading the Gospel more than 30 years after the actual events. They knew that Peter and the other disciples had gone on to establish and grow the early church in spite of persecution. They knew that imperfect disciples could be redeemed and still do God's work.

Notice how Mark interrupts the sayings of Jesus and the narrative of events to explain things for his audience and for us (Mk 1:34). He often includes information not apparent to the participants in the Gospel (like telling us Jesus' thoughts or attitudes during a story in Mk 2:8). *How does this affect the book and our understanding of what is going on? How does it affect your decision to act on what Mark is telling you? Why do you think Mark added these editorial comments?*

Notice how Mark sandwiches episodes together. He will start to tell one story, only to interrupt in the middle and tell another story, before returning to finish the original story. The story of the healing of Jairus' daughter and the woman with a hemorrhage in Mk 5:22-43 is a good example of this. The cursing of the fig tree and the threat about the destruction of the Temple is another example. *Why did Mark sandwich these episodes? We have to remember that Mark chose to put the story about the woman with a hemorrhage in his Gospel.* He could have omitted the story or put it somewhere else. He must have had a reason to include the interruption instead of just finishing the original story.

Mark uses similar episodes to frame sections of his story. Jesus' final trip to Jerusalem starts with a two-stage healing of a blind man in Bethesda (Mk 8:22) and ends with the healing of the blind man at Jericho (Mk 10:46). *Do these healings act as bookends for this section on Jesus' teaching to His disciples? Why is it a two-stage healing in Bethesda and an immediate healing in Jericho? Does it have anything to do with the disciples' imperfect understanding about what it means to be a disciple and Jesus' repeated teachings on discipleship in Mk 8:31, 9:31, and 10:32? Does Mark's sandwich technique help us understand this sequence?* We will discuss these questions in more detail as we go through the text.

Notice the sequence of threes. Some of the sequences are close together (Jesus prays three times in the Garden of Gethsemane) and sometimes the events are spread out over the entire Gospel (there are three episodes of conflict between Jesus and the disciples in a boat and three conflicts with the disciples where the discussion revolves around bread). During the trip to Jerusalem, Jesus predicts His death three times (Mk 8:31, 9:31, and 10:32).

Notice how the disciples react each time and how Jesus patiently uses their lack of understanding as a teaching opportunity. Think a little about the patience of Jesus. **DO THE DISCIPLES EVER "GET IT" IN MARK'S GOSPEL?** They lived night and day with Jesus for three years and still were not sure about Him or what it meant to be His disciple. *What does that mean to us today? Are we any better than the disciples? On the other hand, Jesus used these flawed people as the foundation of His church. Can Jesus still use flawed people to advance His church?*

I know you have too much to think about and notice already, but I have to add a couple of more things to wonder about. This one is more for fun discussion because I don't think there is a definitive answer. OK – here goes. Many people believe that Mark actually ends at Mark 16:8. *Leaving aside for the moment whether this is really the ending or not, why would Mark end his Gospel in such a strange fashion?* The women are scared and run away without telling anyone anything. There are no post resurrection appearances of Jesus with the disciples in the shorter ending of Mark. *Why would Mark end his Gospel this way? If he did end it at Mark 16:8, how does this affect our understanding of his Gospel and what impact would it have had on his original readers?* Remember that his audience was reading the story about 30 years after the actual events and knew what happened to Jesus, Peter and the other disciples after the resurrection.

Finally, notice how Mark "does" theology. He doesn't give us a long academic list of the attributes of God or long discussions on the redeeming work of Jesus as it relates to original sin and eternal salvation. (See, even that sentence was boring and hard to understand.) Mark does theology by telling us a story. It's up to us to be alert and look behind the story for the theological teaching. As you read Mark, always ask yourself what theological point Mark is trying to make. Why did he include this story in this sequence? Notice that Mk 4 ends with a question. Do you think there is a possibility that Mk 5 contains the answer to that question? I promise you that Mark did not slap his Gospel together by accident. Sequence is important.

If you haven't watched the video on honor and shame in the first century, stop right now and go watch it. There will be a link at the end of the chapter for you to follow to find the video. I will wait for you to come back….

OK, great video wasn't it? Well at least I hope so. Now you are equipped to better understand the theology behind the beginning of Mark. Now can you see why Mark establishes Jesus' honor and status with powerful names and important endorsements? Mark names Jesus (at the same time telling us what Jesus' honor status is) in the very first verse of the Gospel. Mark then continues with an Old Testament prophetic endorsement (Isaiah and others), followed by a New Testament prophetic endorsement (John the Baptist). Mark's introduction ends with an endorsement of Jesus by God Himself. God declares Jesus His Son (a very high honor/status position) and then says that He is well pleased with His "Beloved" Son. Not a bad letter of recommendation to appear on your resume. Now ask yourself what kind of theology is behind all of these endorsements. **What do we learn about Jesus as God and Messiah from these quotes?**[3]

Just to show you that I am really sparing you, I won't mention anything about interpreting the parables in Mark or the relationship of Mark's Gospel to Matthew and Luke. That would be an entirely different lesson. Something to stay tuned for.

---

[3] *For fun, watch the first few minutes of the original Godfather movie and see how many honor/shame comments you can catch. I promise you there are a bunch of them.*

Introduction of Blind Bart

Hello. My name is Bartimeus and I share the same name as my father. Sometimes they call me Bartimeus, son of Bartimeus. In order to avoid confusion, my friends just called me "Bart" or "Blind Bart." It was simpler all the way around. When I first heard about Jesus, I was in a desperate situation and had nowhere to turn. I was blind, penniless, homeless and a beggar. I needed a miracle. I heard that a miracle worker claiming to be a descendant of the old Hebrew King David was in the neighborhood and was likely to be coming along the road to Jerusalem. I tried to get in the front row of the crowd waiting for Jesus, but all the people pushed me to the back and told me to shut up. They claimed that because I was blind and couldn't "see" Jesus, it didn't matter if I was in front. After all, He likely wouldn't have time for a blind beggar.

You can read the entire story in Mk 10:46-52, but the important point is that Jesus healed my blindness. Not only was my physical sight restored, but also I received a great spiritual insight at the same time. I saw Jesus for who He really was and immediately decided to follow Him as one of His disciples. I dedicated the rest of my life to helping other "blind" people or people who had questions about Jesus gain a better understanding of who He really is. I will be showing up at various places throughout the book with helpful suggestions or comments. The Jesus that took the time to heal a blind beggar is the same Jesus who is ready to answer your call and restore your sight. My prayer is that you will share in the same miracle that healed me and that you will come to a true understanding of who Jesus really is.

Come, join me as a disciple of Jesus.

ACTIVITIES

Watch the honor and shame video at the following link: **www.BlindBartMinistries.com**.

Questions for further reflection

You may not be ready to fully answer these questions yet, but they are included here for your reference. Go ahead and take a shot at answering them or at least discussing them in a group. Then when you complete your study, come back and see if you answer the questions any differently or in more depth. If you do, then you must have learned something from your study.

1. The first questions you should always ask about the text are as follows. What did Mark include? What was important about the sequence of events? In other words, how does what comes before a particular passage and after that passage have an impact on the meaning of that passage for Mark's audience (and us today)? What does this passage tell about Jesus' nature, mission and character?

2. In your reading of Mk 1, did you notice anything not mentioned in the introduction? What was it and how will it have an impact on how you interpret Mark?

3. If you were going to write a Gospel, whom would you choose as an audience? If you had 16 chapters to tell a particular group everything it needed to know about the life and purpose of Jesus, how would you do it? What would the first and last chapters of your Gospel contain in order to make a great first and final impression? Remember that your beginning sets the stage in the readers' minds for the entire story and your ending will be the last thing in their minds. What are you going to do with your one chance to create a first impression?

4. Who does Mark say that Jesus is? Why do I care about this Jesus? What does this story say about Jesus? What does it say about God? What does it say about our relationship to God and Jesus?

5. Did you find any other occurrences of the "Markan Sandwich?" Why do you think Mark used this peculiar construction? How does the middle or meat of the sandwich help you interpret the bread? We will discuss this in more detail when we get to that section in Mark, but for now feel free to be creative with your reasons for Mark's sandwiches.

6. What is the plot? Who are the characters? What kind of conflicts do they have with each other and Jesus? What is the theme of Mark's Gospel? Why did Mark include the pieces of information that he included and why did he put them in the order that he put them in? (Most everyone agrees that Mark had more material than he used and that Mark did not arrange each piece of his Gospel in exactly the same order they happened in Jesus' life.) Can looking at the sequence of events Mark uses in his Gospel help us interpret his meaning?

7. How does Mark's use of characters, plot and conflict tell us about the person, nature and work of Jesus? Do the characters stay the same or do they develop during the course of the Gospel? Does this development tell us anything about Jesus and the power of the Gospel in our lives? Think how Peter changes from the trial of Jesus to just a couple of months later standing up to the religious leaders who killed Jesus. Was Peter changed by the Gospel, a view of the resurrected Christ and the inspiration of the Holy Spirit?

8. If Mark really does end at Mk 16:8, how do you feel about his ending? Does it leave you hanging? Does it force you to ask more questions about the text and perhaps yourself? Can you think of any reason why Mark might have ended the way he did?

9. What do you learn about Jesus from his three-fold introduction in Mk 1?

The Gospel of Mark

Mark 1: *The Beginning of the Gospel*

- The miracles begin
- Conflict and power themes
- Activities: Questions for further reflection

MARK 1

One of the things you will need to do to effectively study Mark's Gospel is to track the narrative action. I will get you started by giving you an example of the action in Mk 1. You don't need much detail, but the sequence of events is important to understanding Mark.

Narrative Action

    Book Introduction
        As an aside, remember "Good News" or "Gospel" had a secular meaning before it had a Christian meaning.

    Old Testament flashback – Mal 3:1; Is 40:3
        Old Testament prophets' announcement of Jesus

    John the Baptist
        New Testament prophet's announcement of Jesus

    Jesus' baptism and anointing with the Holy Spirit
        God's announcement of Jesus

    Jesus tempted in the wilderness
        Jesus confronted Satan and won

    Jesus picked first four disciples

    Jesus began mission to preach with authority

    Jesus confronted Satan and won again

    Jesus healed on the Sabbath

    Jesus preached and confronted Satan (still the winner)

    Jesus touched, cleansed, and healed a leper

MARK 1: *The beginning of the gospel*

Do you pick up any common themes in the first chapter? For instance, what does it tell us that Jesus can be tempted? More importantly, how does Jesus overcome Satan? Why do you think Mark tells us and shows us these things? What do we learn about the person, work, and character of Jesus? Often Mark tells us something and leaves it up to us to interpret the meaning. The healing of the leper is a great story, but what does it tell us about Jesus? Why does Jesus tell the leper not to tell anyone about the healing? Do you notice that the leper and Jesus change places? Originally, the leper is an outcast that can't come into town because of his condition. Jesus winds up not able to go into town because of His condition. What does the healing and exorcism tell us about Jesus' nature, power, and mission? Do you think it is significant that Mark starts off with the first public miracle of Jesus being an exorcism?

Remember that Mark used action to tell the Gospel story, but he also used the action to tell us theology. *The healing stories are great miracles, but what theology do they reveal? Who and what does Jesus have power over? What does this tell us about God and His kingdom? Hint – is there any sickness in God's kingdom?* Maybe Mark used Jesus' "miracles" as signs of His power and as a glimpse of what His kingdom will be like.

Characters
- John the Baptist
- Jesus the Christ
- Simon, Andrew, James, and John
- Satan and demons
- The people
- The healed people (not named here)
- Narrator
- Reader (original and current)

Watch how these characters interact with Jesus and are changed (or not changed) by their contact with Jesus. What can we learn by how they react to Jesus? What is their understanding of Jesus? What is our understanding of Jesus after one chapter of Mark? Do you see yourself in any of these characters?

Titles of Jesus

Keep track of Jesus' names and titles and see what they tell you about the nature, mission and power of Jesus. Sometimes the titles and names will be clear and sometimes they will be buried in the story. Calling Jesus "demon possessed" doesn't sound like a title, but it is a dirty name that has a deviant status associated with it.

MARK 1: *The beginning of the gospel*

What titles or names for Jesus have we seen so far?

A.	Jesus	Mk 1:1
B.	Christ	Mk 1:1
C.	The Son of God	Mk 1:1; 3:11
D.	My Beloved Son	Mk 1:11
E.	The Holy one of God	Mk 1:25
F.	The Son of Man	Mk 2:10; 2:28

Books have been written and wars fought over exactly what these names mean, but let me summarize some of them. His human name was Jesus or Yeshua in Hebrew. If Mary ever got mad at Jesus as a little boy that is what she called him. If she was really mad, she probably called him Jesus bar Joseph (Jesus son of Joseph).[4] The name "Christ" means Messiah or "anointed one" and is used in the Old Testament to refer to kings or priests or anyone anointed for God's special purpose. Even Cyrus, a pagan king, could be called God's anointed one or messiah (Is 45). The difference was that Jesus was "The Messiah," not a messiah.

The title Son of God indicates that Jesus is fully God. Jesus, as a human, still participates (in some way I don't understand) fully in the nature of God. Jesus is God and this title shows this to us. People in the first century (Jewish and Roman) thought that the son was always the exact representation of the father and spoke with all the authority of the father. We still do that today when we say, "Like father, like son." Jesus as the Son of God directly represented God, spoke with all His authority, and literally was God.

The title Son of Man was Jesus' favorite way to refer to Himself. This title shows us that Jesus was fully human. He was born of a human mother and grew up experiencing things like any other young Jewish boy. This is very important. Only God become human could provide a sacrifice big enough to take away all the sins of all humanity for all time. Jesus was fully human (so He can understand all our temptations) and fully divine (so He never sinned and remained a pure unblemished sacrifice). Jesus was God's method of removing the burden of sin from any person who accepted Jesus as his Savior. See how much theology can be in a title? Use a concordance or Bible software to look up the Old Testament references to the Son of Man and see what you think they mean.

---

[4] *Yes, I know it should be Jesus bar Holy Spirit, but Mary lost track of her theology when she was mad.*

MARK 1: *The beginning of the gospel*

There are two major Old Testament usages. Make sure you find both of them. *Can you see why this was Jesus' favorite title? What implications did it have?* If you don't find the references, ask someone else in your group. Understanding the Old Testament background of this title will be important to understanding how Jesus presented Himself to His world.

The miracles begin - 1:21-28 - Exorcism as Jesus' first miracle

First occasions are always important and are the things we tend to remember. You may remember your first bicycle ride, your first car or even your first kiss. In his Gospel, Mark did something unusual by describing an exorcism in a synagogue as Jesus' first miracle. The synagogue was a public place of worship and teaching where everyone came together to celebrate the community of God.

The synagogue in Capernaum where Jesus taught and exorcised a demon.

Exorcism is not something we are familiar with or even comfortable with today, even though it appears often in the Gospels. Mark must have thought that Jesus' exorcisms conveyed an important message for his original audience or was at least something they should know about. Perhaps the question we should ask today is, *"What do these exorcisms tell us about Jesus, His work and His nature?"* After all, wasn't that Mark's purpose in writing his Gospel to his original audience and why we still read his Gospel today?

To a person in the first century, demons and demonic possession represented the unpredictable and the uncontrollable forces of chaos. A possessed person was literally out of his mind, beyond the control of any human power and a danger to everyone around him. The possessed person became the physical manifestation of the demonic forces. To encounter a possessed person was to be in the presence of demons and demonic forces.

The Korazin synagogue – notice the steps leading up to the synagogue are uneven. You were forced to slow down and approach reverently as you climbed up to the synagogue.

Amateur and professional exorcists were familiar and popular showmen in the first century, and the process was seen as a battle between the forces of good and evil. The exorcism itself normally consisted of the exorcist attempting to learn the demon's name and then using that name along with incantations invoking various gods' names in order to force the demon out of the possessed person. The incantations would be accompanied by vivid gestures, smoke, incense and anything else extraordinary the exorcist could think of to impress his audience and the demon being exorcised.

The point of the entire exercise was that the exorcist had no real power to get rid of the demon. He had to depend on the power of the demon's name or the power of the gods to actually remove the demon. Whoever was "stronger" would win the contest and demonstrate his authority over the demonic forces of chaos. The story about the Sons of Sceva in Acts 19:13-16 showed what happened when the exorcist lost the power battle.

One clue that Mark gave us about the purpose and meaning of our passage was the use of the word "authority" in Mk 1:22 and 27, at the beginning and ending of the passage. The people of Galilee recognized Jesus as an authority different from the Scribes, who claimed authority based on the Scriptures or what we would call the Old Testament. For example, a Scribe might quote passages from Genesis or Exodus as authority for his position on what kind of activities could properly be done on the Sabbath. Jesus apparently claimed His own authority as a basis for teaching, rather than just depending on the Scriptures. Matthew gave us a picture of Jesus doing this in the Sermon on the Mount when Jesus told the people that they had "heard" in reference to Scripture, but that He was "saying" to them what the Scripture actually meant (Mt 5:21-22).

Once inside the synagogue, there was plenty of room for the entire community to meet.

A claim to that kind of authority required some kind of proof before people would consider it authentic. After all, they had depended on what the religious leaders told them about the Scriptures for thousands of years. What kind of authority did this Jesus have to reinterpret what they had been taught?

It may not show up in your translation, but Mark made a point of Jesus *immediately* starting to teach once He arrived in Capernaum and that once Jesus started teaching, the demonically possessed man *immediately* interrupted Jesus. In essence, the demon challenged Jesus' power and authority to teach about the Kingdom of God. The confrontation was set. The only question was, "Who would have the most authority or power?"

The seat of honor at the synagogue in Korazin. Either the worship leader or the visiting dignitary would sit here.

The differences between a normal exorcism and Jesus' exorcism were immediately clear. The demon correctly identified Jesus and may have tried to use Jesus' human name (Jesus of Nazareth) and His Divine name (Holy One of God) as a means to control Him. In other words, the demon tried to establish his power over Jesus just like he had established his power over the possessed man. One might wonder if the demon thought he could "exorcise" Jesus' Holy nature out of His human body. If this was the case, the demon was immediately put in his place.

Jesus used none of the tools of the normal exorcist. There were no incantations, calling on the authority of others, smoke, gestures or even anything attention gathering. All Jesus did was speak, command the demon to be silent, and come out of the man. There was no real contest here, and Jesus didn't have to work up a sweat to exorcise the demon. All it took was a word of power from the Son of God and the demon immediately obeyed Jesus. If nothing else, this passage reminds us today of the awesome power of God's word. The world was created by a word from God and if the book of Revelation is correct, the world will be ended and recreated by a word from God. Mark showed Jesus controlling the demon by His own authority and at the same time answered the question about what kind of authority Jesus had.

The only thing the demon could do to demonstrate his frustration was to throw the man into convulsions and then leave him. The demon did nothing to Jesus except obey Him. Mark didn't tell his audience what happened to the demon or the man, because that wasn't the purpose of his story. The point of the story was to demonstrate Jesus had the authority to command and control the forces of evil and chaos in the world. In the immediate context of the story, Jesus had the power to save a man from the forces of evil. Later in Mk 5, the story of the Gerasene demoniac showed how Jesus could not only free a man, but also restore him to his proper spiritual state and send him out to tell others what God had accomplished.

What does this all mean to us today? First we have to remember that names still have the power to label us and carry the responsibility to live up to that name. Jesus claimed authority as the "Son of God" and the "Holy One of Israel" and demonstrated that He had that authority by controlling the demonic forces of evil. Today we are called Saints, the holy ones (of God), Children of God and Christians. How should we live in demonstration of exactly what those names mean? Jesus was faithful to His titles. Will we be faithful to ours? If you were accused and on trial for being a Christian, would there be enough evidence to convict you? Jesus knew God's purpose for His life and fulfilled it. Will we do the same?

If even the Son of God has His teaching interrupted and His commitment tested by demons, why should we think that we would be treated any differently? *If we are fulfilling God's purpose, how long will it take Satan to try and interfere with us? How might we see that working in our lives today?* One thing that Mark never did in his Gospel was underestimate the power of evil. Mark showed demons having the power to control people and destroy their lives, but Mark also showed that power disappearing in the presence of Jesus. It may be reading too much into the story, but while demons can't control Christians, they can throw us into convulsions. Evil is still present in the world, and we are called as Christians to live our lives in opposition to that evil. As we do that, we confirm our reputation as children of God and live up to God's purpose for our lives.

Conflicts and Power Themes

Jesus showed His power to heal and forgive sins. **Notice** how Mark showed Jesus immediately demonstrating His name and power. Jesus called people and exorcised demons. He healed people and this caused Him to be in conflict with the religious establishment. *Why would Mark put this conflict so early in his Gospel? For that matter, why would Mark emphasize conflict from the very people who were best qualified to recognize and follow the Son of God? What was Mark trying to show his audience with this conflict? Did these people reject Jesus on the evidence before them or were they too proud and arrogant to accept what they saw and heard?*

The Pharisees were a Jewish denomination that believed that the way to holiness was by works and they considered themselves "the holy ones of God." They had an incredibly complicated system of over 600 laws that had to be obeyed perfectly. They believed that if they followed all these laws they would be blessed by God and would not sin. They were very zealous and sometimes were even self-righteous. They believed the only way to please God was to follow all the laws and sacrifice regularly at the Temple. For Jesus to claim to be able to forgive sins directly was a slap at all they held holy. If Jesus were correct, they would have to give up a great deal of what they thought was holy. *Did the Pharisees let what they "knew" get in the way of what they were experiencing? Did their arrogance keep them from seeing the truth? What does our arrogance blind us about today?*

MARK 1: *The beginning of the gospel*

ACTIVITIES

Questions for further discussion or reflection

1. What do the miracles tell you about Jesus, His power and the kingdom of God? How did the people react to the miracles? Did they see them as signs pointing to the nature of the kingdom of God or did they see them as free food and healing?

2. Do you pick up any common themes in the first chapter? For instance, what does it tell us that Jesus can be tempted? More importantly, how does Jesus overcome Satan? Why do you think Mark tells us and shows us these things? What do we learn about the person, work, and character of Jesus? Often Mark tells us something and leaves it up to us to interpret the meaning.

3. The healing of the leper is a great story, but what does it tell us about Jesus? Why does Jesus tell the leper not to tell anyone about the healing? Do you notice that the leper and Jesus change places? Originally, the leper is an outcast that can't come into town because of his condition. Jesus winds up not able to go into town because of His condition. What does the healing and exorcism tell us about Jesus' nature, power, and mission? Do you think it is significant that Jesus' first public miracle in Mark was an exorcism?

4. What else does the story about Jesus and the leper tell you about Jesus? Why was He not rendered unclean after He touched the leper? Why would He tell the leper to be announced "clean" by the High Priest before he did anything else?

5. Watch how the characters interact with Jesus and are changed (or not changed) by their contact with Jesus. What can we learn by how they react to Jesus? What is their understanding of Jesus? What is our understanding of Jesus after one chapter? Do you see yourself in any of these characters?

6. Why do you think that Mark used an exorcism as Jesus' first miracle in his Gospel?

7. What does this all mean to us today? First we have to remember that names still have the power to label us and carry the responsibility to live up to that name. Jesus claimed authority as the "Son of God" and the "Holy One of Israel" and demonstrated that He had that authority by controlling the demonic forces of evil. Today we are called Saints, the holy ones (of God), Children of God and Christians. How should we live in demonstration of exactly what those names mean? Jesus was faithful to His titles. Will we be faithful to ours? If you were accused and on trial for being a Christian, would there be enough evidence to convict you? Jesus knew God's purpose for His life and fulfilled it. Will we do the same? If we are fulfilling God's purpose, how long will it take Satan to try and interfere with us? How might we see that working in our lives today?

8. What characters do you identify with the most in this chapter? Do they change based on their interaction with Jesus? Can you put yourself in their places and determine if you would act any differently? Would you leave your day job just because someone told you to follow him? What would be enough to make you do that?

9. What did you discover about the use of the title "Son of Man" in the Old Testament? Which of the two meanings do you think Jesus intended when He used the title? Was this a way that Jesus could announce His true mission to "those who could hear" and conceal it from "those who remained deaf?" If Jesus had publically claimed to be the end times Son of God, what do you think the Jewish people and the Roman soldiers would have done?

10. Why does Mark introduce the conflict theme so early in his Gospel and why do you think most of the religious leadership is in such conflict with Jesus? For that matter, why would Mark emphasize conflict from the very people who were best qualified to recognize and follow the Son of God? What was Mark trying to show his audience with this conflict? Did these people reject Jesus on the evidence before them or were they too proud and arrogant to accept what they saw and heard?

The Gospel of Mark

Mark 2: *The Beginning of the Conflict*

- The confict deepens
- New wine and old wineskins
- The conflict turns deadly
- Activities: Questions for further reflection

MARK 2

The Beginning of the Conflict: Healing the Paralytic – Mk 2:3-13

Mark wrote his Gospel to answer questions his audience had about Jesus. One of those questions might have been, "Why aren't more Jews becoming Christians? After all, weren't they closest to Him and knew Him best?" Mark's audience might also have been interested in why so many Jews and Jewish leaders were actively opposed to Jesus. I believe that one of the main lessons here is in Mk 2:10, where Jesus claimed to have the power to forgive sins. To the watching Pharisees this was clearly blasphemy and was punishable by death under Jewish law.

Today it is hard for us to understand the power and impact of this statement. Other Old Testament prophets had healed and performed miracles, but the Jews believed that only God could forgive sin. Rather than seeing Jesus as God, they saw Him as a threat to their system and their own status. As self-appointed protectors of their religion, it was up to them to silence Jesus' heretical preaching and make sure no one else spread His message. If Jesus were lying, they would have been correct in their actions.

(Sermon warning) Jesus was not blaspheming, because He was not lying. He did have the power to forgive sin. Today, Jesus also has the power to forgive sin. There is nothing we can do that Jesus cannot forgive. Our problem is that we often don't forgive ourselves for our sin or we don't forgive others for their sins. The answer to all forgiveness of sin is Jesus. He forgives our sin and He gives us the power (through the Holy Spirit) to forgive others for their sins against us. OK – the sermon is over. Feel free to take up a small collection and we can move on.

Notice that the paralytic's friends brought him to Jesus. Notice Jesus healed his spiritual and physical needs. *Why do you think Jesus forgave the paralyzed man's sin before He dealt with his physical problem? We all need friends and we all need to be friends to others. Who around you needs physical or spiritual help? What are you doing to help them?* We all have our laundry list for prayer, but maybe we need to add something to our prayer list. Maybe we need to ask Jesus whom we need to help. Ask in prayer and then listen for an answer. Be alert. God may give you a name or He may put someone in your life. If He does, be sure to do something about it.

Also **notice** that these four friends went to a fair amount of trouble to get the paralytic to Jesus. We may be asked to carry another's burden for a while or we may be asked to dig a hole in the roof for someone else. Ask yourself, *"What is God calling me to do?"* Be ready for an answer and be ready to be obedient. We may also be called to sacrifice our earthly goods for someone else. Always remember that the roof that was destroyed belonged to someone who was very happy to have a full roof over his head. In healing the paralytic, he lost his roof. How do you think he felt about that exchange? OK – Now the sermon is really over. Maybe. For a while.

The Conflict Deepens: Eating with Sinners, Tax Collectors, and Sabbath Rules – Mk 2:15-28

The Pharisees had very strict rules about whom they could eat with and what they had to do before they could eat. Jesus eating with sinners and tax collectors pretty much broke all those rules. This passage pointed out the difference between Jesus and the Pharisees and explained why they were so aggravated at Him. The healing on the Sabbath was important, but the important thing here is to see that Jesus was in conflict with the established religious leadership of His day.

Jesus asked some very important questions about the Law and the Pharisees' religious beliefs. They did not like to have their accepted wisdom challenged and I suspect we still don't like our accepted wisdom challenged today. As you read and meditate on Mark's Gospel, ask yourself which of your accepted beliefs are being challenged. The question was whether Jesus was speaking the truth. If He wasn't, He deserved punishment as a heretic. If He was, then everyone's life was overturned. Would they be able to stretch and accept this new teaching?

New Wine Into Old Wineskins – Mk 2:21-22

Wine was often fermented and stored in new goatskins. A new skin could expand with the fermentation of the wine and contain the wine without bursting. An old wine skin lost its ability to expand and would be destroyed. *Do you get Jesus' point? To whom was Jesus talking? What* was the context of the discussion? What was His point? Read Jn 3:1-21. Pay special attention to Jn 3:3-7 and 3:16-17. Read Gal 2:20. How do these passages apply?

Questions to think about. *What kind of old patches do we still have on our new bodies? What kind of old baggage are we still carrying around that keeps us from stretching and accepting God's word?* If you have been asking God for something and have not received it, maybe the reason is that your old wineskin won't hold it. Ask God to totally transform you into what He wants you to be. Then be ready to be filled with God's new wine.

Spend some time pondering Mk 2:27-28. *How would a first century Jew have reacted to Jesus' comment? Watch how the titles work. What was Jesus claiming? Was this "Son of Man" title really just referring to Himself as just a son of a man? How would Mark's audience have reacted to this teaching?* Remember that if Mark wrote to Rome in the early 60s AD, his audience would have contained many Christian Jews and might have met in Jewish synagogues. Lots of opportunity for conflict.

The Conflict Turns Deadly – Mk 3:1-6

I include this material in Mk 2 because it is the climax of the early conflict stories. Mark worked up to this punch line to set the stage for the more serious conflict that will happen once Jesus reached Jerusalem.

Now they really got mad at Jesus. Here was Jesus healing again on the Sabbath and He had the chutzpah (a good Jewish word) to do it in church. The Pharisees got so mad they started talking about killing Jesus. It's only the third chapter of the book and they are contemplating murder. Notice with whom they ally themselves. Remember that the Pharisees wrapped themselves in the Law as a way to live and keep themselves separate from the Romans. The Herodians had gone the other way and become almost Roman in their desire to accommodate themselves to their Roman masters. Does their alliance strike you as very strange? In modern terms it would be like the KKK working with the Nation of Islam in order to kill the Pope. (Maybe not the world's best example, but I hope you get my general meaning.)

MARK 2: *The beginning of the conflict*

ACTIVITIES

Create a narrative outline of the chapter, a list of the characters and a list of the titles used in the chapter. Refer back to the sample in Chapter 1 if you need a review of the format.

Questions for further discussion or reflection

1. It is easy to criticize the Pharisees for denying the evidence before them and rejecting Jesus. But are we any different today? As Christians, we accept as true the evidence of the Bible, but do we really live our lives based on that knowledge? Do we accept God's teachings that allow us to remain as we are or do we accept the uncomfortable teachings that force us to grow in our love for others and God? What parts of the Bible do you understand and accept as truth that you have trouble following?

2. Why do you think Jesus forgave the paralyzed man's sin before He dealt with his physical problem? What friends do you have that need some help in order to be healed? How is Jesus calling you to help them? So often in the Bible, groups of people do things together. Who is in your group? What kind of things should you help each other with?

3. If you were the owner of the house with a new and unexpected skylight, how would you react? Would you expect some kind of recompense? If you were the friends of the paralyzed man, would you hang around to fix the roof? Why didn't Jesus miraculously restore the roof? Maybe Jesus did. Just because Mark didn't include it, doesn't mean that it didn't happen.

4. Do some research and see if you can determine why the Sabbath was such a big deal to the Pharisees. What was Jesus' opinion about the Sabbath? How do you think that applies today? For that matter, what is the "correct" way to celebrate the Sabbath today? What should Christians do or not do on the Sabbath?

5. OK, everyone agrees that the Pharisees had lost track of what was important in religion. Today, what have we lost track of? Do we ever stray over into self-righteous legalism or miss the true message of Jesus?

6. People in the first century had to stretch to understand the message of Jesus and follow Him. Is there anything today in Christ's message that we can't stretch to accommodate? Does what we have been "told" is true ever get in the way of accepting what is really true about Jesus? Do you have any early lessons you need to unlearn? What does the Biblical text actually say as opposed to what you have been taught it says? As a hint, Jesus had to adjust people's opinions about God's true intent in the Sermon on the Mount in Matthew's Gospel.

7. Is there any doubt in your mind about your personal salvation? Relax, I am not going to ask you the famous, "If you died tonight, do you know where you would go" question. Personally, I would probably go to the hospital and then the funeral home, but that would just be a stop on my way to heaven.

If you are starting to get the feeling that you are a sinner and need forgiveness, God may be working on your heart. It may be time for you to go with Jesus, even if the world tells you He is crazy. If you admit that you are a sinner, if you repent of your sin and if, in faith, you accept Jesus as your Lord and Savior, you can be saved immediately. The process is simple because God takes care of it for you. Doing it is hard because in our arrogance we do not want to be totally dependent on God. If you have questions about this, please ask your group leader, professor or even send me an email at **jmorris@point.edu**. Any one of us would love to talk to you about this.

The Gospel of Mark

Mark 3: *The Real Family of Jesus*

- Jesus picks His disciples to be with Him
- Jesus' family tries a forceful intervention
- The unpardonable sin
- Activities: Questions for further reflection

MARK 3

The Real Family of Jesus

Two very strange things happen narratively in this chapter. The first is that Jesus chooses a group of men to become His disciples. Disciples normally chose a teacher, but in this case Jesus does the calling. In the context of the chapter, these people will become His new family in contrast to His old family, who is in the process of rejecting Him. Family in first century culture was incredibly important. You protected the honor and status of your family even if it meant that you suffered personally. I don't want to go too far here, but Mark may be making some more statements about the nature of the Kingdom of Heaven.

The Jews were by birth included in the "family" of God. They even called themselves the children of God and claimed the privilege to address God as "Father." In many cases, their lives revolved around their special status as God's children. If you wanted to join the family, like Ruth or Rahab in the Old Testament, you had to become Jewish. In Mark, Jesus calls people to be in His family regardless of birth. People who don't know Him accept the call of discipleship and become part of His (God's) family. Birth members of His family reject Him and are no longer part of the family. Mark showed Jesus emphasizing this in Mk 3:33-35. Anyone, even Gentiles, could become part of the family.

What would this mean to Gentiles in the first century? Think about people who had been rejected, like lepers, women with hemorrhages, the Ethiopian eunuch, and the Syrophoenician woman. Now they could join God's family and share the same family status as the Jews without becoming Jewish. *What do you think this means for us today and does it have any impact on how we see denominations or protect our own denomination?*

MARK 3: *The real family of Jesus*

Jesus Picked His Disciples to Be with Him – Mk 3:13-19

What did Jesus do in this passage? Why did He do it? **Notice** that Mark gave us two reasons. I believe that the order of the reasons is important and indicated Jesus' priorities. First, the disciples were called to be with Him and then second, to preach. I believe this is incredibly important for us today. The Pharisees were trying to please God by doing. Jesus called His disciples (and us today) to "be" with Him first and then "do" as He directed. Unless we are first with Him, we can do nothing to please Him. Once we are with Him, He will tell us what to do.

This is subtle, but **notice** what Jesus does not tell them to do. There was no preaching about Jesus the Messiah, overthrowing the Roman Empire, or initiating the Kingdom of God. While this passage did not mention the subject of their preaching, the second time Jesus sent the disciples out preaching, He specifically told them to preach a message of repentance – exactly the same thing John the Baptist preached.

If we haven't "been" with Jesus sufficiently to become like Him or understand exactly who He is, should we be careful what we preach?

From a cultural point of view, Jesus acted exactly as a first century person undergoing a reputation attack was expected to act. Mark showed the Pharisees and Herodians getting together in order to attack Jesus and kill Him. Their first step was the same as it is today. You destroyed the person's reputation by getting a group of influential people to disparage the person you were trying to attack. If they had enough credibility (gravitas in today's terms) people would start to believe their accusations. Once the public started believing one bad thing, they became willing and maybe even eager to believe any number of bad things about the person.

Today, once we hear that someone is arrested, we assume he or she must have done something wrong. Otherwise the police wouldn't have arrested the person. If a person is convicted of a crime, we wonder what other crimes they committed, but didn't get convicted for. The first century defense to this kind of reputation attack was to gather together a group of influential friends and have them go out and start spreading the good news about your reputation. Think about today's talking heads or spin-meisters.

The Herodians and Pharisees had their group, so Jesus called His group. I do not think this was the only reason Jesus called His disciples. I definitely think He had a kingdom purpose for them, but it is interesting how Jesus' kingdom purpose fit so well within the social norms of the first century. Jesus followed some social norms by calling disciples (defenders), but He also broke away from the acceptable pattern.

The people Jesus called weren't powerful, well known or good speakers. They were common people. Jesus didn't send them out to defend His reputation, but instead apparently told them to preach the same message of repentance that John the Baptist preached. As we get deeper into Mark, we may think that the reason Jesus didn't want them preaching about Himself or the Kingdom of God was because they really didn't understand the true nature of these Kingdoms. Until they really understood what they were preaching about, Jesus didn't want them to deliver a confusing or contradictory message.

Jesus' Family Tries a Forceful Intervention – Mk 3:20-35

Mark shows us something very strange here in order to introduce the concept of family in the Kingdom of God. I think we might have a little bit of the classic Markan sandwich. Mark starts one story about Jesus and His family, changes the subject in the middle to show Jesus defending Himself against the charge of being demon possessed, and then returns to a discussion about family. We will spend more time on this "sandwich" technique when we get to Mk 5. For now, **notice** what is going on and be ready to think more about it later.

Normally in the first century, a family discussion would have preceded any kind of story about a person. Note that Mark showed us Jesus' heavenly Father, but no real mention of Jesus' earthly family. Now we get to see who they are. **Notice** until now that Jesus' family has had no trouble with His popularity or His actions. Remember that Mark has emphasized how large the reputation of Jesus has gotten. So many people were following Him that He couldn't get into town because of the crowds. Apparently Jesus' family had been content to enjoy the reflected glory.

But now, in Mk 3:21, Jesus came home and all of a sudden the family was ashamed of His actions and was ready to perform an intervention. Mark hid a very serious action in some simple words. Jesus' family tried to go out and "take custody" of Him because they thought He was crazy. In essence, they were going to take Him out of the public realm and hide Him away in the attic because they were ashamed of Him. They even gave Him the shameful title of being "crazy!" Remember individual shame hurt the entire family. They thought it was a better tradeoff for people to think that there was insanity in the family rather than whatever it was that Jesus was doing to make them uncomfortable. Rather than supporting Him, Jesus' family had started to attack Him and His reputation.

MARK 3: *The real family of Jesus*

What had Jesus' family heard in Mk 3:21 that spurred them into action? While there is no way for us to determine today exactly what set Jesus' family against Him, there are clues in the text. Mk 3:20 mentioned that Jesus and His disciples were so busy that they didn't even have time to eat. Given how little food everyone had, perhaps they thought that anyone who was too busy to eat had to be crazy. 😎

More likely the issue revolved around Jesus' exorcisms and the charge that He was demon possessed. Mark used the same Greek word to describe what his family did to Him (take custody or literally "possess") as he did to describe the charge the people from Jerusalem made against Jesus (He was demon "possessed"). They charged that the only way Jesus could control demons was that if He Himself were demon possessed. In essence, they denied that Jesus performed His miracles and signs through the power of God. Instead they claimed Jesus used the power of Satan. Jesus defended Himself with the familiar parable and showed that He was indeed in His right mind and not possessed by any demon.

As an aside, notice that the people from Jerusalem never questioned whether Jesus could perform all these miracles. They just questioned where His power came from.

The Unpardonable Sin - Mk 3:29

This is sometimes called the "unpardonable sin." Be ready to discuss this in the "Questions for further discussion" section.

ACTIVITIES

Create a narrative outline of the chapter, a list of the characters and a list of the titles used in the chapter.

Questions for further discussion or reflection

1. If you had to choose a group of people to be your disciples and spread the good news about you, whom would you choose and how would you choose them? Would you pick people who were already masters at what you needed, or people who could become what you needed through God's changing power? How would you get them to follow you?

2. Think about examples today in the media where the general public rushed to judgment before all the facts were discovered. If you were living in the first century, which version of the facts about Jesus would you believe? Today, what misinformation is in the media about Christians and how can you combat the false information? Should you try to infiltrate the media with Christian influence, set up a separate Christian media or just try to show a Christian lifestyle to the world? Which do you think would be most effective?

3. Today, do we ever feel like we have to lock up Jesus in the attic like a crazy old uncle? Are we ashamed of the Gospel and what it means to us in our daily lives? Has there ever been a time in your life when you wished the whole "Christian" thing would just go away? Describe that time and explain how you got through.

4. What do you think the unpardonable sin is? Does it still apply to us today and does it apply to believers and non-believers? Is this a sin that we can do today? **Notice** the context of this comment. Who was Jesus talking to? Of what have they just accused Him? Of what did the unpardonable sin really consist? Be sure to read Mk 3:30 along with Mk 2:29. How does this apply to us today?

5. Think about the dynamics of understanding that Jesus really can perform miracles that demonstrate He has the power of God's Kingdom, preaches a perfectly orthodox message about repenting and preparing for God's Kingdom, and only claims to be a son of man? How blind would you have to be not to pay attention to Him and follow Him? How could so many people be wrong? In the same light, given that we know even more about Jesus today, how can we not believe and be enthusiastic followers of Him and His way?

The Gospel of Mark

Mark 4: *Jesus Teaches in Parables*

- Devotion - The parable of the four soils
- Devotion - In waters just like these
- Activities: Questions for further reflection

MARK 4

Jesus Teaches in Parables

This chapter of Mark is full of parables. A parable is a teaching story or illustration and was a popular Jewish teaching technique. Typically a parable had just one point even though that point sometimes might not show up until the end and was often unexpected. In some cases, a parable could have multiple points depending on the audience. For instance, the meaning of the parable of the prodigal son can depend on which son you identify with. Parables often used metaphors like seeds, lamps, coins or harvests. A parable did not have to be true or filled with real characters, but it reflected reality and had a strong teaching lesson. The parable used some familiar situation in the life of the hearers and the situation's meaning to them. The parable's lesson could be unexpected or even hard to understand. On the other hand, if the parable was directed against a group like the Pharisees, they often understood exactly what Jesus was trying to communicate (Mt 21:45).

Parables made people think about what the meaning really was and gave the hearers an easy way to remember the lesson. Parables also gave people the freedom to not understand. You could "hear" a parable and still "not hear" the parable. In other words, "Those who have ears, let them hear." (Mk 4:9) To really "hear" a parable implied that you understood the meaning and would obey the teaching.

In the first parable of the soils, apparently no one understood what Jesus was saying. *Did you understand His message? What does it mean to you? Why would Jesus tell a story with a point that was hard to understand?*

What influences people? Does God plant seeds in people's lives? Does the devil also plant seeds or does he just plant weeds? Do people plant seeds in each other's lives? Did you ever stop to think about how you got to where you are today? What have been the major influences in your life?

Notice how Jesus' power worked. He commanded demons, the weather, sickness and even death and they all instantly responded to His power.

MARK 4: *Jesus teaches in parables*

Mark showed Jesus occasionally commanding people, but the people often directly disobeyed Jesus. Jesus' normal style in Mark was to teach truth to the people and then leave the reaction up to the people. It appeared that people in Mark are able to reject Jesus. *Do you wonder what that says about the unpardonable sin and how it applies to us?*

Parable of the Four Soils – Mk 4:1-22

The first step in analyzing or understanding a parable is to ask, *"Who is the audience?"* Read this parable closely and see if you can determine the audience for this parable. The answer is in the Biblical text, but it might not be what you are expecting. The main question you need to ask is, "Is the audience believers or seekers?" Your answer will have an impact on how you understand the parable.

Are these four soils representative of four ways people respond to God's message? Do you think the parable is evangelically directed at non-believers or teaching directed towards those who already believe? Could the parable be about how people respond differently at different times in their lives or in different areas of their lives? Are you starting to see the power of parables? Sometimes seeds have to stay hidden in the ground for a long time before they sprout and produce a harvest. Are all the areas of your life the same? Do you have some fertile ground and some stony ground that you refuse to turn over to God?

Based on reading the end of the chapter, what kind of soil do you think the disciples were? What does that mean for you? Do you think you can do better than the disciples? Before you are too hard on the disciples, remember they gave up everything to faithfully follow Jesus. They may have occasionally failed, but they never gave up. They tried their best to develop their faith and be true disciples of Jesus. Does Jesus ask for perfection or faithful following and your best effort? Do you begin to see why Mark emphasized the difficulties the disciples had to overcome? Remember that Mark wrote to an audience who was probably facing persecution and dealing with their own failure as disciples. Also remember that Mark's audience knew what happened to Peter and the other disciples after their own initial failure. Fallible disciples who were forgiven and later went on to be powerful figures in the church was a great example for Mark's persecuted and fallible audience. The same applies to us today.

Looking back on how you got to where you are today, what seeds were planted in your life? Who planted them? Did they grow or were they destroyed in some way? Did they produce a harvest? What kind? If you were going to plant some seeds today in others, what kind of seeds would they be?

MARK 4: *Jesus teaches in parables*

If you were going to plant some seeds in yourself, what kind would they be? How do you plant seeds?

What kind of soil are you right now? What kind of soil would you like to be? What is keeping you from being that soil? What are you going to do about it?

What are the cares of this world specifically? What do we use to drown out God's word? Where do we go to look for satisfaction? Did you ever say, "I will be happy if only I can get a _____?" Were you happy for very long after you got it?

Spend some time alone and in quiet this week. Ask God what seeds He has planted in your life. Ask Him for help in becoming fertile soil. Pay attention to what He says and be ready to faithfully follow Him. Remember that weeds grow every day and have to be constantly removed. *What weeds do you have growing in you that are drowning out God's word?*

Mk 4:23-24 is the secret of being fertile ground. Listen to God. Be obedient. Decide to give up whatever you need to give up and follow Him faithfully. God rewards our least effort. Go back and look at what the people in the first three chapters had to do to be healed. They did not have to be perfect. They did not even have to be particularly faithful. All they had to do was approach Jesus and ask to follow Him. All they had to do was take the first step. Pick one seed and try to be fertile ground in the coming week. The growth and harvest is up to God. I believe the meaning of Mk 4:26-29 is that if you make yourself receptive, God will cause growth and manage the harvest.

We are all at different points in our relationship with Jesus and God. But we are all in the same situation. God is waiting for us the take the next step. God will respond to the smallest baby step with His Love and Grace, but He will not force us to move our feet.

Mk 4 ended with Mark switching from the viewpoint of Jesus' teaching to the perspective of the disciples. Don't be fooled; the teaching hasn't stopped. Only the method has changed. Mark taught his audience by telling them a story and asking questions. *Notice* how Mk 4 ended with the question, *"Who then is this?" Notice how the titles and actions of Jesus in the next chapter answered the questions. What do you think the stories in Mk 4-5 tell us about Jesus and the disciples? If you had to decide on the point of the stories, what would it be – faith, fear, or what kind of man Jesus really was?*

Read the following short devotion about Jesus teaching on the Sea of Galilee and be ready to reflect on what it means to you today.

MARK 4: *Jesus teaches in parables*

Mk 4:35-41 - Sea of Galilee - "In Waters Just Like These"

The gap between Mount Arbel on the left and the hills on the right is where big storms descend without warning onto the Sea of Galilee.

There are many places in the Holy land that claim to have a connection to Jesus, but few of them are as certain as the Sea of Galilee. At the Temple foundation in Jerusalem, you can take your shoes off and walk on the same pavement that Jesus walked on almost 2000 years ago. On the Sea of Galilee, you have the opportunity to "float" where Jesus floated.

I once helped deliver a sailboat from the factory in Florida to St. Thomas in the Virgin Islands. To save money, the delivery skipper used amateur sailors instead of a paid delivery crew. Rather than give us a long safety lecture that we would probably ignore, he had a different method to teach us what we needed to know. To make sure we paid attention during the long night watches alone at the helm, he would entertain us with us stories while we ate dinner. Each story would start with the quote, "It was in waters just like these." He would proceed to tell us a story about when he was first mate on a freighter carrying dynamite with a drunken captain. He would tell us about getting up in the middle of the night and discovering the skipper passed out drunk at the wheel and the freighter just about ready to run over some poor, dark and unsuspecting sailboat – "in waters just like these." During our night watches, you can rest assured that we were always on the lookout for that dynamite boat and its drunken skipper.

MARK 4: *Jesus teaches in parables*

First Century fishing boat from Galilee

It wasn't "in waters just like these," it was in *these* waters, on this lake that Jesus worked with the fishermen, used it as a way to conveniently travel around the area, and occasionally escaped from the crowds by taking a boat out onto the water. With cities dotted all around the lake, using a boat to travel directly to the "other side" was much easier than walking around the entire lake. In the same way, a boat trip from city to city on the same side of the lake was easier than walking up and down the mountains surrounding the lake. In a way, this was Jesus' interstate highway without speed limits or traffic jams. Given this ease of travel, information about a new healer who was giving away free food could travel very quickly.

It's hard not to think of the Sea of Galilee in terms of metaphors of life. The Sea normally appears calm and peaceful, but meteorologists today also tell us that it can turn violent, dangerous, and life threatening with very little warning. As you float here, you don't think about the hundreds of feet of space between yourself and the bottom and what might be in that space – much like our subconscious minds. Floating here you feel peaceful and in control of your life - "in waters just like these."

It was on a calm night that Jesus told His disciples that He wanted to leave the Jewish side of the sea and go over to the Gentile side (Mk 4:35-41). In the dark, the disciples didn't see the storm coming over the mountaintops, but they noticed when the storm-generated waves started filling up the open boat. As it so often happens, life caught them by surprise. What started as a short commute to a new teaching location turned into a life or death experience – "in waters just like these."

MARK 4: *Jesus teaches in parables*

At the time, Jesus had spent a long day teaching the crowds and His disciples about the Kingdom of God. Like any teacher after an all-day class, Jesus was tired, but hopeful that His students had learned what He had been trying to teach. Resting from His labors, He was taking a nap in the stern of the boat. As the storm hit and the boat filled with water, the disciples turned to the only help they knew – Jesus. The disciples confronted Jesus as He was sleeping not with a plea to be rescued, but with an accusation that Jesus didn't care that they were in deadly peril. How could their "teacher" and Savior let something like this happen to them? They blamed Jesus for their own situation and not really caring about them. *Do we ever accuse Jesus about the same thing today?*

Jesus didn't have any trouble dealing with the life and death situation. He got up (hard to do in a storm-tossed boat), rebuked the wind, told the sea to "Hush and be still," and it did! Jesus then asked His disciples two questions. Why were they afraid and why did they *still* have no faith? From a teacher's point of view, Jesus was really asking His disciples why they hadn't learned anything from the day's teaching. It must have been very frustrating for Jesus to have taught His best and still be surrounded by disciples who didn't understand their teacher's lesson – "in waters just like these."

The punch line to the whole story might be how it ended. The Greek literally said, "They feared a great fear." The disciples were afraid when they woke Jesus up, but they really panicked when they saw what Jesus could do. They were afraid because they didn't know what kind of man they were following. All of a sudden whom they were following was much more important than a sinking boat. The dangers of this life paled before the awesome (and fear producing) nature of the God they followed – "in waters just like these." [5]

Are we any different than Jesus' disciples? How often do we accuse God of not being concerned about the real dangers and perils we face in this life? How often do we blame God for the problems we have? Do we ever want God to wake up and take care of our peril? Do we ever expect God to

---

[5] *Your view of the nature of Christ will determine how you follow Him. If your view of Him is just someone who can rescue you from problem situations, you aren't likely to follow Him through a bad situation. You are likely to abandon Him in the middle of the situation. Christians follow a Christ who stays with them during the persecution and trials even if He doesn't always deliver the people from the trials. The seven churches in Revelation were undergoing intense persecution and you may wonder where Jesus was in the midst of this persecution. The initial vision in Revelation showed that Jesus was in the middle of the seven churches and with them in their persecution (Rev 1:13).*

magically solve all the tribulations we have in this life? God will sometimes still the waters of our life, but that is not the most important aspect of His love for us. The question He asks us today is the same question Jesus asked His disciples. *"Why are we afraid, and why don't we have faith in Him?"* Why don't we have more faith in God? We can look down on the disciples because they didn't understand who Jesus was and were afraid in a situation that we know wasn't really dangerous. We know the story ended safely. But are we any different today - "in waters just like these."

God does care that we are perishing – just like the disciples in these waters. The unfortunate news is that perishing is a part of this fallen world. Evil is always present, even if it is hidden under the surface of our lives or the surface of this water. Sometimes that evil threatens to pain us or kill us. Jesus' message is that in the midst of that danger and pain, He is in the boat with us. We are not alone in our peril. Jesus can stand in the midst of the storm and He has control over all the forces of this world. If we understand what being in the Kingdom of Heaven really means, we understand that this stormy world can do no lasting harm to us. It can cause us fear, pain, and even kill us, but God through Jesus has an eternal solution to all problems. God is in control even of something as fear producing as death.

When we are in fear, pain, and tribulation, we should ask ourselves, "Who is this that we are following and why don't we have more faith?" The more we learn about whom we follow, the greater our faith should become, and in the same way, the less our fear should be - "in waters just like these."

P.S. As lagniappe, Mark's story of the Gerasene demoniac in Mk 5 answers the question the disciples ask at the end of Mk 4. "Who is this guy?"

MARK 4: *Jesus teaches in parables*

ACTIVITIES

Create a narrative outline of the chapter, a list of the characters and a list of the titles used in the chapter.

Questions for further discussion or reflection

1. In the first parable of the soils, apparently no one understood what Jesus was saying. Did you understand His message? What does it mean to you? Why would Jesus tell a story with a point that was hard to understand?

2. Are these four soils representative of four ways people respond to God's message? Do you think the parable is evangelically directed at non-believers or teaching directed towards those who already believe? Could the parable be about how people respond differently at different times in their lives or in different areas of their lives? Are you starting to see the power of parables? Sometimes seeds have to stay hidden in the ground for a long time before they sprout and produce a harvest. Are all the areas of your life the same? Do you have some fertile ground and some stony ground that you refuse to turn over to God? Are there weeds in your life that need to be pulled out?

3. What influences people? Does God plant seeds in people's lives? Does the devil also plant seeds or does he just plant weeds? Do people plant seeds in each other's lives? Did you ever stop to think about how you got to where you are today? What have been the major influences in your life?

4. Looking back on how you got to where you are today, what seeds were planted in your life? Who planted them? Did they grow or were they destroyed in some way? Did they produce a harvest? What kind? If you were going to plant some seeds today in others, what kind of seeds would they be? If you were going to plant some seeds in yourself, what kind would they be? How do you plant seeds?

5. What are the cares of this world specifically? What do we use to drown out God's word? Where do we go to look for satisfaction? Did you ever say, "I will be happy if only I can "get a _____?" Were you happy for very long after you got it?

6. Mark taught his audience by telling them a story and asking questions. **Notice** how chapter 4 ended with the question, "Who then is this?' **Notice** how the titles and actions of Jesus in the next chapter answered the questions. What do you think the stories in Mk 4-5 tell us about Jesus and the disciples? If you had to decide on the point of the stories, what would it be – faith, fear, or what kind of man Jesus really was?

7. What weeds do you have growing in your life? What kind of harvest are the weeds destroying? Do you need to do some "weeding" in your life?

The Gospel of Mark

Mark 5: *The Question Answered: Who Is This That Even the Wind and Sea Obey Him?*

- Gerasene Demoniac
- Activities: Questions for further reflection

MARK 5

The Question Answered: *Who Is This That Even the Wind and the Sea Obey Him?*

In chapter 5, Jesus again showed He had power over demons and even death.

Gerasene Demoniac – Mk 5:1-20

The disciples had just seen Jesus calm the waters of the Sea of Galilee and in Mk 4:41, they asked about what kind of man Jesus was. Mark answered that question by telling the story of the Gerasene demoniac and laying the theological meaning underneath the entertaining story. So what kind of man was Jesus that He had power over natural and unnatural forces? *What theology do we learn from the story?*

First, Jesus was the kind of man who was willing to leave the religious isolation of the Jewish side of the Sea of Galilee and reach out to the Gentiles on the other side of the sea. A "proper" Jew would never do this and would travel miles out of his way to avoid the Gentiles on the Eastern side of Galilee.

Second, Jesus was the kind of man who not only commanded the uncontrollable forces of a natural storm on the sea, but he also commanded the demonic forces that occupied a man and turned him into something that no human being could control. The danger of confronting the demon-possessed human threatened Jesus no more than confronting the life-threatening storm. In one respect, the atmospheric storm on the sea was paralleled by the demonic storm in the possessed human.

Third, Jesus was the kind of man whom the demons recognized as the "Son of the Most High God" – a powerful title in the first century where Caesar was a god and Herod fell down dead after he allowed a crowd to say that his voice sounded like, "The voice of God" (Acts 12:22). In the culture, if you allowed someone to call you an honorable or shameful title and didn't respond to the name, it meant that you accepted the burden of honor or shame attached to that name. It was dangerous to claim an honor that you didn't deserve.

The disciples may not have known what kind of man they were following, but the demons had no trouble at all recognizing who Jesus was. In fact, they recognized Jesus from a distance and came running to Him in order to bow down before Him. The disciples followed Jesus without having a clear idea of who He was, while the demons knew exactly who Jesus was and refused to follow Him. The Gerasene demoniac recognized, submitted, and correctly named Jesus. If there were any doubt about how to answer the question asked in Mark 4:41, the Gerasene demoniac answered it.

Fourth, Jesus was the kind of man who could banish an entire "legion" of demons. Jesus didn't have to work up a sweat to control and banish the demons. The demons clearly recognized Jesus' power and superiority. All the demons asked was an opportunity to get away from Jesus by being transported into a nearby herd of pigs. It might be reading too much into the Mark story, but the irresistible and uncontrollable Roman Legion, which was occupying Palestine as conqueror, used a boar on its flag. Was Mark saying that Jesus was also the kind of man who could control and expel the Roman Legion as easily as He controlled and exorcised the demon named Legion?

Fifth, Jesus was the kind of man who could deliver humans from all natural and unnatural oppressive forces. Jesus was the kind of man who could take the worst that Satan and his demonic forces could do to destroy a human being and restore that person to his proper mental and physical state. The man who started the story as an uncontrollable wild man ended the story as a rational, well dressed man who wanted to follow Jesus.

Sixth, Jesus was the kind of man who could charge a person to go and tell what God had done for that person. Jesus refused to allow the cured Gentile man to accompany Him back to the Jewish side of the Sea of Galilee – perhaps because a Gentile would not be an acceptable witness on the Jewish side of the sea. Instead, Jesus told the Gentile man to go back to his home and tell everyone there what God had done. Apparently the man was successful in his mission because the next time Jesus passed through the Decapolis area, the people there expected Jesus to be able to perform miraculous healings.

Finally, Jesus was the kind of man who when you encountered Him and accepted Him as your leader, you left behind what you thought was important and accepted Jesus' values. If you stuck to the world's values of the demonic legions, you would have an uncontrollable life of confusion and strife. If you called yourself a Christian, you accepted God's values and led a life of forgiveness, restoration and reconciliation.

MARK 5: *The question answered*

ACTIVITIES

Create a narrative outline of the chapter, a list of the characters and a list of the titles used in the chapter.

Questions for further discussion or reflection

1. What kind of person do you think Jesus is? What does that mean to you as you live your life today?

2. Remember that everyone was terrified of the demoniac. Is it possible that God is calling you to cross your own Sea of Galilee and witness about what He has done in your life to someone that you are not comfortable with? Is your fear limiting what God wants you to do?

3. Do you think there are demonic forces at work in the world today? Do you see their influence anywhere? Do you think demons still exist? Why do you think demons appear so often in the Gospels, but not in our daily life today?

4. Can Christians be possessed or can demons just do their best to undermine a Christian's life?

5. What does it mean to accept God's values in your life and to lead a life based on those values? Be honest. If you really adopted all of God's values, how would your life be different today? The real question is how soon are you going to change?

6. Why didn't Jesus just destroy the Roman legions as easily as he destroyed the demonic legions? What does this tell us about God's Kingdom as opposed to Caesar's Kingdom? (Hint: the Sermon on the Mount in Mt 5-7 spends a lot of time contrasting God's and Caesar's kingdoms.

The Gospel of Mark

Mark 6: *The Conflict Returns*

- Jesus feeds the people in the wilderness
- Activities: Questions for further reflection

MARK 6

The Conflict Returns

Jesus in Nazareth - Mk 6:1-6

Long before Jesus got in trouble for preaching the presence of the Kingdom of God in Jerusalem, He got in trouble for doing the same thing in Nazareth. Long before they tried to crucify Him in Jerusalem for claiming to be God's Son, they tried to kill Him in Nazareth. We obviously don't know exactly where it happened, but the Jezreel Valley overlook in the picture below is certainly close.

Matthew, Mark and Luke all showed Jesus being tempted in the wilderness somewhere close to the beginning of their Gospels. Immediately after this temptation, Jesus began to preach and be recognized as a teacher in the synagogues. His teaching amazed the people because Jesus didn't

Nazareth Overlook

MARK 6: *The conflict returns*

Modern Day Nazareth

speak like all the other scribes or Pharisees who depended on someone else's authority as they taught the Bible. Jesus interpreted and spoke using His own authority. Eventually, He came to Nazareth, and as was normal for a visiting Rabbi, He was invited to expound on a passage from Isaiah at the synagogue there.

Mk 6:1-6 and Lk 4:16-19; 24-27

The Spirit of the Lord GOD is upon me,
Because the LORD has anointed me
To bring good news to the afflicted;
He has sent me to bind up the brokenhearted,
To proclaim liberty to captives,
And freedom to prisoners;
To proclaim the favorable year of the LORD. (Is 61:1)

Luke did not record if Jesus read the remaining part of Isaiah or just assumed that His audience would be familiar with the passage, but he does say that Jesus' reading spellbound the people. How could someone they knew read the Scripture with such grace and power? So far so good as far as they were concerned. A local boy does good.

Then Jesus went from preaching to meddling by comparing His ministry to Elijah and Elisha's – prophets who lived in Northern Israel. These prophets, as Jesus reminded His audience, had cared about people other than just the Jews. God called Elijah to feed a poor Gentile widow and her family and even bring her son back from the dead. As a result the widow acknowledged that Elijah was a truthful man and a man of God. Then the woman said to Elijah, "Now I know that you are a man of God, and that the word of the LORD in your mouth is truth" (1Kgs 17:7-24). Elisha offered healing to a Gentile leper, who was the captain of the King's army. As a result, the Gentile acknowledged God as the only God and refused to worship His king's god. In each case, the recipient of the miracle acknowledged the accuracy of the prophet and the authority of God.

Something about these passages filled the people in the synagogue with rage, and they tried to lynch Jesus by throwing Him over a cliff similar to the one pictured above.

Part of the problem may have been that they thought they knew who Jesus was – the son of Mary instead of the son of Joseph or some other man (Mk 6:1ff). The normal and honorable way to refer to Jesus would have been to call Him Jesus bar Joseph or Jesus, son of Joseph. Calling Jesus the son of Mary may have been a way to call to attention the controversy about whether Joseph was really Jesus' father or not. Even worse than being the son of an out-of-wedlock father was not even knowing who your father was.

The first century was a time and culture of blatant stereotypes. People thought that if they knew who your father was and where you were from, they already knew everything about you that was needed to reach decisions about what kind of person you were. We still have some similar attitudes today when we say the "acorn doesn't fall far from the tree" or that "like father, like son." Unlike others, they couldn't criticize Jesus for being from Nazareth (nothing good ever came out of Nazareth), but they could question whether Jesus even knew who his father was.

Everybody in Nazareth thought they "knew" exactly who Jesus was. He was Mary's boy. They could look at His brothers and sisters who were sitting around Him. Couldn't they remember when He and His "father" came back from Egypt and set up shop in Nazareth? Who did Jesus think He was to start interpreting the Scriptures on His own authority, and claiming that He was the fulfillment of some passage from Isaiah? That wasn't bad enough. Then He went on to remind the people from Nazareth that He wasn't the first prophet who cared about non-Jewish people and that He intended to do the same thing as Elijah and Elisha.

MARK 6: *The conflict returns*

View from the Nazareth Overlook of the Jezreel Valley

View from the Nazareth overlook of Mount Tabor: the assumed site of the Transfiguration of Jesus.

That sacrilegious message might go over in heathen places like Galilee, but the "righteous and orthodox" people of Nazareth weren't going to let that nonsense infect their town.[6]

Today, how often do we think we know who Jesus is and how does that have an impact on our lives? How often do we think we can ignore something from God because we don't want to obey or learn the lesson that He is trying to teach us? Have we ever tried to "throw Jesus off the cliff?"

If Mk 5 was the good example of what can happen when people believe in Jesus, Mk 6 was the bad example of what happens when you don't believe in Jesus. If you reject His Kingdom, like His family did in Mk 6:1-6, you don't see the "signs" of the Kingdom (miracles). In Mk 6, Jesus faced reverses caused by men. His family and neighbors rejected Him, and His mentor (John) was killed. The chapter ended with two of the most well known miracles of Jesus - the feeding of the 5,000 (the only parable or story that is included in all four Gospels) and Jesus walking on water. Notice in Mk 6:52, His disciples still didn't get it. The man who could control all natural forces was portrayed by Mark as apparently not able to control human beings.

Jesus Feeds People in the Wilderness - Mk 6:34-44

Notice how the feeding came at an inconvenient time. It was late and in the middle of nowhere. Jesus had been teaching all day and was probably tired, yet His disciples came to Him with one more problem. Jesus always seemed to have time for their problems. He never complained when His disciples brought Him problems. He occasionally asked some tough questions, but He never complained. Notice that He always delivered when their request was Godly and valid. The disciples claimed that they didn't have the resources to do God's work of feeding the people.

Do we ever claim that we are too busy or don't have the resources to do God's work? Will God ever ask us to do something without giving us the resources with which to do it? OK, dumb question, but I hope you get the point. Now that you "get" the point, will you do anything about it? Just a thought for reflection.

---

[6] *The Jewish religious leaders in Jerusalem did pretty much the same thing to Stephen in Acts 7:58-60. A violent response to God's word was not limited to small country towns. I love the part where the Jewish leaders stick their fingers in their ears and make a loud noise so they don't have to hear Stephen. I can just see them screaming, " Nah, Nah, Nah. I can't hear you," and yes I think Luke deliberately portrayed them as two year olds.*

MARK 6: *The conflict returns*

The disciples were indifferent to the hungry people. They wanted to send them away, but Jesus apparently felt compassion for the people because they were sheep without a shepherd. Read Psalm 23 and think about what kind of shepherd Jesus might be. Use the concordance in the back of your Bible and look up other references to "shepherd." Think about other instances where a man interceded with God and food was provided to a multitude. Does this sound like Moses and manna in the wilderness? Can you begin to see why people might think of Jesus as the new Moses or Elijah?[7]

Notice how much Jesus does with just a little bit. *If we take the time in our busy lives when it is inconvenient and care about people, if we give Jesus just the little bit we have, look what He can do. What is Jesus waiting for us to give Him for His work?* Think about how this applies to the parable of the mustard seed. The smallest seed can produce a great shade tree. In these times of great pain and trouble, when we definitely need a shepherd to lead and protect us, don't forget that Jesus is just waiting for us to give Him what we have. If we do that, He will produce great miracles. **Notice** that where He was rejected (in His homeland) that He performed few miracles. This doesn't mean that He couldn't produce miracles because of His neighbors' lack of faith, but it could mean that Jesus was not going to force Himself onto those who rejected Him. Remember, those who have ears, let them hear.

If you have time, read about the other two times God or Jesus fed the people. Many people think the feeding of the 5,000 Jews resembled God feeding manna to the Jews during the Exodus and foreshadowed Jesus and the Last Supper.

As a side note, Jesus was an equal opportunity feeder. The 4000 people that Jesus later fed were apparently Gentiles. We assume this because Mark used a word that specifically referred to baskets Jews would use when he recorded feeding the 5000 and baskets Gentiles would use in feeing the 4000. If nothing else, think about what a wide separation there must have been between Jews and Gentiles if they had different words for their carrying baskets.

Mark ended chapter 6 with stories about the disciples and the crowds that showed that neither of the two groups really understood who Jesus was and why He had come to earth. The people focused on Jesus the miracle worker who could heal and feed them on the physical level rather than

---

[7] **Notice** *the topic of the preaching in this chapter. It is exactly the same as the sermons of John the Baptist.*

the Son of God who could heal them on a spiritual level. It was fun to follow this miracle worker and be the recipient of free food. Even though Jesus was being misinterpreted by all of the people, His popularity was becoming a danger to the established religious leadership.

Mark's summary indicates that the disciples' lack of understanding paralleled the crowd's view of Jesus. Although the people immediately recognized Jesus, they were more concerned with what He could do for them than with His identity or mission. The image Mark created of Jesus walking up and down long lines of sick people lying on their cots awaiting healing has a contemporary flavor of wounded warriors waiting for triage and treatment. Mark immediately pointed out how Jesus' increasing popularity created more conflict, this time with the Pharisees and Scribes who had traveled from Jerusalem. Jesus was no longer a local phenomenon in remote Galilee. Now, Jesus had attracted the attention of the urban leadership.

MARK 6: *The conflict returns*

ACTIVITIES

Create a narrative outline of the chapter, a list of the characters and a list of the titles used in the chapter.

Questions for further discussion or reflection

1. Do we ever claim that we are too busy or don't have the resources to do God's work? Will God ever ask us to do something without giving us the resources with which to do it? OK, dumb question, but I hope you get the point. Now that you "get" the point, will you do anything about it?

2. Think about other instances where a man interceded with God and food was provided to a multitude. Does this sound like Moses and manna in the wilderness? Can you begin to see why people might think of Jesus as the new Moses or Elijah?

3. In the feeding miracle, what Jesus did with the faith of one person and just a little bit of food. Is there a message there for us today about what God can do with our small offerings? What do you think Jesus is waiting on for you to give Him so He can perform a miracle?

4. Why do you think the disciples had such a hard time understanding exactly who Jesus was? Do we suffer from the same problem today?

5. Are there problems in the world that you are indifferent to today? What do you think Jesus would say and do about those problems? More importantly, what do you think Jesus is asking you to do about those problems? (Reading the Bible can get awfully personal and confrontational can't it?)

6. Many of us have spent decades as Christians and have come to believe that we know exactly who Jesus is. Do we really know Him that well or do we just know what our churches have told us about Him? Are our preconceived notions about who Jesus is keeping us from experiencing the miracles of God's kingdom? This is why I am such a big proponent of reading the Biblical text and discovering exactly what it says.

The Gospel of Mark

Mark 7: *The Conflict With the Pharisees*

- Conflict with tradition
- What really defiles a person
- Jesus and the Syrophoenician woman
- Activities: Questions for further reflection

MARK 7

The Conflict With the Pharisees

Notice in Mark 7 that the story starts to move from the power of Jesus over evil and the things of this world to His conflict with people. While Jesus may have had conflicts with evil, the conflict was very short and always resulted in Jesus being victorious. You have to ask yourself why Mark so consistently portrayed Jesus that way. *What does it say about Jesus, His mission and the kingdom of heaven?*

Conflict with tradition – Mk 7:1-17

Now back to the conflict. Make a list with whom He gets into a conflict. *What is the conflict over? Or as Emma, my wife, would prefer, over what is the conflict?[8] What was the real purpose of God's purity laws? How does God really want to be honored? Have you **noticed** that in Mark, Jesus apparently has complete power over everything other than human beings?* The weather, demons, sickness, natural laws, and even food perfectly understand who Jesus is and obey Him. Only humans have trouble understanding who He is and following His teachings. It is not until His crucifixion that a Roman centurion correctly names Jesus as the Son of God. I don't want to jump ahead, but think about what it must have meant for someone who worked for and was paid by "the son of god" (namely Caesar) to say that Jesus was truly the Son of God!

One of the defining characteristics of Judaism in Roman society was that it followed God's commandments. Even if people knew nothing else about Judaism, they knew about circumcision and following the Law. As new or seeking Christians, Mark's audience may have wondered why Christians didn't follow all the old Jewish laws. (They were probably so happy to get a pass on the whole circumcision thing that they didn't question other Jewish laws.)

---

[8] *She reminds me that I should never end a sentence with a dangling participle, or maybe it's a preposition.*

Mark may have used these stories of Jesus' confrontation with the Pharisees to answer his audience's questions and to show them that it was perfectly allowable not to be saddled any longer with the Law and to address the issue of defilement. **Notice** that Mark included an editorial comment about all food being clean in Mk 7:19. This was another issue that probably concerned his Gentile audience.

Notice the charge and response in Mk 7:8-9. These were serious accusations, since not following the Law could result in ostracism from Judaism or even death. Jesus defended Himself and showed how the Pharisees destroyed tradition by bending the Law to suit their own selfish purposes. Jesus in essence said that they were guilty of the very indiscretion they were accusing Him of and gave the Pharisees a strong example of how they broke their own Law. Jesus then gave the crowd a piece of new teaching about the real intent of the Old Testament Law. Jesus did the same in His teaching about the healing and eating grain on the Sabbath in Mk 2. The Sermon on the Mount was even more consistent with this pattern by showing Jesus teaching that, "You have heard it said, but I say." (Mt 6)

The Gospels made clear that Jesus didn't come to destroy the Law but to fulfill it. The Pharisees and others of Jesus' time had manipulated the Law so extensively that they had lost track of what God meant by giving them the Law. For instance, over the centuries, they had developed rules of great detail over what constituted "work" on the Sabbath. They had decided that lighting a fire was work and therefore forbidden on the Sabbath. You could keep a fire going, but you couldn't start one without it being work. If you needed a fire that badly, the Pharisees decided you could always hire a Gentile to start the fire for you. Of course, if you did that, you had the whole impurity thing to deal with. I don't say this to make fun of the first century Jews, but I use it as an example of how thoroughly they had entangled themselves in the Law. What was meant as a blessing from God had become a yoke and a burden.[9] Jesus pointed out that even the Law had exceptions for unusual or dangerous circumstances. (Mk 2:24-28)

What Really Defiles a Person? - Mk 7:17-23

Jesus talked about the things that really do defile us. How many of them are you guilty of? The legalistic Jews of that time did not focus on their

---

[9] *You see similar things today on ovens with "Sabbath clocks" that can be set to turn on at a certain time. In Israel today, pushing elevator buttons constitutes work, so on the Sabbath, all elevators stop on every floor. In some hotels, they have Gentile elevators for the non-Jews who don't want to stop on every floor.*

thought lives but on their actions. They believed that if they lived right and followed the 600+ laws, they were right with God regardless of what was in their hearts. Jesus said that no amount of actions could clean you if your heart was defiled. Defilement came from the inside not the outside. We are condemned by our minds and not by our actions. By the same token, we are saved by repenting of our sins and giving our lives to Jesus. Both of these actions are emotional and mental, not physical. Physical action comes out of our salvation experience, but is not the source of our salvation.

This idea of an internal state being more important than following ritual was not something new in the New Testament. Many of the Old Testament prophets carried the same message (Amos 5:21-27). Jesus said the same in the Sermon on the Mount when He said that being angry with your brother was as bad as murder (Mt 5:21-22).

What kind of inner thoughts are defiling you? Those thoughts keep you from a closer relationship with God and keep you from receiving all the blessings He wants you to have. What are you going to do to discourage those thoughts?

The Syrophoenician Woman - Mk 7:24-30

Notice that after this talk about purity, Jesus goes from "pure" Jewish territory to "impure" Gentile territory. *The Syrophoenician woman and the feeding of the 4,000 all take place in Gentile territory. Did Jesus really call this woman a dog? How did she react? How would you have reacted? What was the woman willing to sacrifice to get her daughter healed? Was her faith rewarded?*

Go back and make a list of the Gentiles that Jesus heals or provides for. I will give you a hint to get you started – one instance includes 4,000 people. While Jesus came to His own people first, He always had time for the Gentiles and sometimes directly sought them out. Here is another hint. The Sea of Galilee was divided into Gentile and Jewish territory. In general, the East side was Gentile (think the Decapolis) and the West was Jewish. When Jesus "crosses over to the other side," He is moving from Jewish to Gentile territory or the reverse. *Notice that Jesus had contact with the unclean (lepers, demons and Gentiles) without Himself becoming unclean. What do you think this said about Him and His kingdom? What is real purity and where does it come from?*

MARK 7: *The conflict with the Pharisees*

ACTIVITIES

Create a narrative outline of the chapter, a list of the characters and a list of the titles used in the chapter.

Questions for further discussion or reflection

1. Why do you think Mark showed Jesus having so many easy victories over the forces of evil? What does that say about Jesus, His mission and the kingdom of heaven? Do you notice that Jesus apparently doesn't control human beings? He directs people to do things and sometimes they don't do them. Do you think Mark is making a point there? What do you think it means to us today?

2. Now back to the conflict. Make a list with whom He gets into a conflict. What is the conflict over? What does the conflict tell us about Jesus and His relationship to the world? What does that tell us about what our relationship to the world should be? What was the real purpose of God's purity laws? How does God really want to be honored?

3. Jesus talked about things that really defile us. How many of them are you guilty of? What kind of inner thoughts are defiling you? What are you doing to discourage those thoughts?

4. What is real purity and from where does it come? How can we live a pure life in an impure world?

The Gospel of Mark

Mark 8: *Jesus Teaching How to Be a Disciple*

- Feeding the Gentiles in the wilderness
- Who is Jesus and what does it mean to be His disciple?
- Peter's confession of Christ
- Activities: Questions for further reflection

MARK 8

Jesus Teaching How to Be a Disciple

The Third Gentile Miracle - Mk 8:1-10

Chapter 8 started with the miracle of feeding the 4,000. While it is hard to tell from the text, it appears that the 4,000 are Gentiles. The general narrative location was in Gentile territory with the story of the Syrophoenician woman and the geography of the Decapolis. Mk 8:10 told of another boat trip and then mentioned Pharisees, implying that Jesus returned to Jewish territory. There was also an implication in the miracle that the Greek word referring to the baskets full of leftovers referred to Gentile baskets as opposed to the Greek word used to refer to Jewish baskets in the feeding of the 5,000.

If the feeding of the 5,000 is somehow connected to the manna in the Exodus, the Passover, and the Last Supper, what does it mean that Jesus provides the same miracle for Gentiles who are also seeking Him? Could God's blessings and provisions also be for Gentiles? Mark seemed to say that the answer was "Yes."

Mark finished this section on teaching of the kingdom with a depressing summary in Mk 8:11-12. Even after all the teaching Jesus had completed, the Pharisees still didn't get it. The disciples didn't get it. Even the entire generation didn't get it. Obviously something else needed to be done to help at least the disciples understand who Jesus was, why He came, and what it meant to be His follower (disciple). Jesus actually went on a small rant asking them how they could have experienced everything they saw and still not understand (Mk 8:21). My prayer is that Jesus never says something like that to me, but I am afraid that He does it every day and will continue to do so. Are we still looking for signs? Is our faith based on a continuous stream of miracles? How can we have read what we have read, seen what we have seen, and still not understand who Jesus is and what it means to follow Him?

Mk 8:18 is one of the few specific Old Testament references in Mark's Gospel and quotes Isaiah describing a generation who refused to listen to God's prophet. From the perspective of Mark's audience, would they make the same mistake? From our modern perspective, will we make the same mistake?

Who Is Jesus and What Does it Mean to Be His Disciple? - Mk 8:21-26 (A blind man can "see" the answer, even if it takes him a while.)

Mark brought us to a strong climax in Mk 8:21 about the lack of understanding and then changed the theme and subject – or did he? The two-stage healing of the blind man was a strange miracle by any account. *Was the healing so difficult that Jesus couldn't do it all at once? Why does Jesus ask the blind man if he can see after the first partial healing? Does the miracle have any connection to what just happened and what will happen in the next few chapters? Who is this Jesus and what does it mean to be His disciple?*

Let me give you a couple of hints. First, in the Gospels, physical blindness is often associated with spiritual blindness. Understanding what you physically see is often equated with understanding what you spiritually experience. Remember that Jesus was the light of the world who came to defeat the darkness. Now, go back and read Mk 8:21. Is Jesus' question to the blind man the same kind of question as Jesus asked the disciples? Second, there are two healings of blind men coming up in the next few chapters of Mark. In between the two healings is a series of sections where the disciples demonstrate they don't know what it means to be a follower of Jesus and then Jesus gives them some strong teaching on exactly what it means to be a follower of Jesus.

Now let's summarize. Mark shows us a miracle that implies partial understanding or growing understanding (vision), shows Jesus teaching about what it means to be a disciple (to disciples who only partially understand what Jesus is teaching about discipleship) and ends with the restoration of vision to Bartimaeus (who appears to become a disciple of Jesus). I wonder if Mark did that on purpose?

On a completely secular level, Jesus' two-stage healing duplicates what happens in real life when someone who was previously sighted (the blind man knew what trees looked like) regains his sight. The nerves and physical connections may be restored, but the brain no longer understands how to interpret the new vision signals it is getting. People with cochlear implants may have perfectly restored hearing connections, but they still have to learn how to "hear" again. Jesus cures the man's eyes and then he heals his understanding (physical and spiritual maybe?).

MARK 8: *Jesus teaching how to be a disciple*

I think the climax of Mark happened in Mk 8:27-37. The question in Mark was always "Who is Jesus?" The challenge was always "What do I do with this knowledge?" Read through this passage several times and meditate on it. *Notice what is happening and think about what it means. What happens in the passage immediately before Mk 8:27? Is this a strange kind of healing story? Go back and reread some of the other healing stories. It turns out that they follow a fairly regular pattern. Does this story follow the same pattern? Why would Mark include this story and why would he include it here? Why do you think it follows a different pattern? What does it mean to us today to be a follower of Jesus?*

Up until now in his Gospel, Mark showed Jesus teaching about the Kingdom of God but not a lot about what it means to be a member in that kingdom.[10] *Mk 8-10 appears to spend a great deal of time on the subject. Do you think it was something Mark's audience needed to know? How about us today?*

Before this passage, Mark did not include a lot of the teaching of Jesus. Then right after Jesus accepted the designation of Messiah in Mk 8:29, He started teaching some painful lessons. Remember, Jews were looking for the Messiah to be some kind of military leader and savior who would kick the Romans out of the Promised Land and restore the Jews to their rightful place of world leadership. This is not how Jesus described His role.

I believe that the first part of Mark describes who Jesus was and why we need to follow Him. I believe the second part of Mark tells us what it means to be a follower of Jesus and how we must follow Him. Ultimately, we need to be ready to follow Him even if it means being faithful until death. From a broader perspective, it means we have to be ready to more than die for Jesus. We need to be ready to live for Him in the way that He wants us to live. Sometimes facing the day-to-day world as practicing Christians can be harder than making a one-time instant decision to die for Him. Living for Him can get very tiring in the day-to-day world.

The second part of Mark is no easier for us to accept than it was for the early disciples. Remember that today we are all still disciples of Jesus. As we finish Mark, think about what it really means to be a disciple of Jesus. How do you need to change your life to become a better disciple of Jesus?

---

[10] This may by why Matthew started his Gospel with the Sermon on the Mount which clearly spelled out what a member in God's kingdom would be like.

MARK 8: *Jesus teaching how to be a disciple*

Why do you think the chapter ends with Jesus talking about shame? Do you think that He thought the disciples were ashamed of Jesus as the "Son of Man?" Were they ashamed to be His disciples if He wasn't going to assume the title of Messiah? Were they ashamed that they had given their entire lives to someone who was going to be condemned and killed as a politically subversive deviant and criminal? Are we any different today? How do we shame Jesus with our actions or thoughts today? If you are ashamed of Jesus, will you lose your soul to the world? What does it mean in today's terms to not be ashamed of Jesus? How does a true disciple live today?

Peter's Confession of Christ - Mk 8:27-33

"Sticks and stones will break my bones, but words will never hurt me," unless the media drags my name through the sewer and everyone believes I am guilty. Then, I can never retrieve my good reputation.

Why does Jesus care about what people think? Isn't any publicity good publicity? What is Mark trying to accomplish in this section?

Peter's confession of Christ is probably one of the most important naming passages in Mark, but the way Mark presents the actions raises many questions. *Why does Jesus ask what other people think about who He is and then ask the disciples who they think He is? If Peter correctly identified Jesus with the title of Messiah, why would Jesus tell the disciples not to tell anyone? Weren't the disciples supposed to be Jesus' witnesses in the world? And finally, why would Jesus publically rebuke Peter by calling him "Satan" and say that Peter's interests were opposed to Jesus' plans?*

I think the answers to all these questions can be answered by understanding the importance of a person's reputation in Jesus' time and culture. As it turns out, the process of naming and the defense of one's reputation works pretty much the same way today. All you need to do to see this in action is to watch any political campaign and how it uses the media to control the candidate's image. The actual truth is less important than what everyone thinks is the truth. If the campaign can get the general public to think their candidate is honest and their opponent is a lying, unpredictable, no good so and so with parents who probably weren't married, they have won the reputation battle. The slandered opponent may bring his religious leader, the pastor that married his parents, and his family to his defense, but once the public has made up its mind, it takes a lot to change it.

MARK 8: *Jesus teaching how to be a disciple*

While you may think the insults and slanders of modern politics are terrible, they don't hold a candle to what was common and accepted in the first century. Some of the first century political insults would curl your hair. A typical insult might run along the lines of, "I would never accuse my opponent's mother of having sex with chickens, but I will note how much his nose looks like a beak and all of his brothers and sisters perch in trees when they go to sleep." Even if the attacked person proved who his father was, people were still going to look at him and his mother with a different viewpoint. They would probably said things like, "Well you know, his toes really do look like he could perch in trees and his mother really does kind of bob her head when she walks."[11]

In the first century, as today, names had power. You were who people said you were, not who you said you were. As an example, even after all of Jesus' teaching to the multitudes, Jesus never overcame the stigma of his early home in Nazareth, because everyone knew, "Can any good thing come out of Nazareth" (Jn 1:46). In the culture, people thought that if they knew who your father was and where you were from, they had a pretty good handle on your personality, status and potential. A person had to publically earn the right to change his inherited status.

Jesus demonstrated this cultural prejudice when He asked His disciples who the people thought He was (Mk 8:27). The disciples reported what they heard and told Jesus that people thought He was John the Baptist or maybe even Elijah. In other words the mass of people in Galilee thought that Jesus was a prophet. This was certainly an honorable title, but was only partially correct. The general populace had heard the teaching but not yet understood exactly who Jesus was. The public had a confused vision of the entire truth. Remember that this passage was introduced by a two stage healing where the blind person initially saw partially and then fully (Mk 8:22-26). **Notice** that Jesus' reputation was not based on being "like" John the Baptist or Elijah, but that Jesus "was" John or Elijah.[12] Most public figures would be happy to bask in the glory of prophetic reputation, but Jesus went one step further to make His question very personal. Jesus had to be very careful that He did everything He could to get the people to understand who He really was instead of who they thought He was.

---

[11] *Songs about Julius Caesar joyfully and habitually receiving homosexual advances from a foreign king were rampant and incredibly popular during and after his life. And yes, the songs were much cruder and explicit than my description. By the way, almost any kind of sexual activity was acceptable for a Roman man as long as he was the aggressor. The Roman shame in the first century was not being the aggressor or not being in control of the relationship.*

[12] *Herod the Tetrarch thought that Jesus was John the Baptist reborn (Mk 6:14-16 and Mt 14:1-2).*

MARK 8: *Jesus teaching how to be a disciple*

Jesus then asked His disciples who they thought He was (Mk 8:29). This forced the disciples to not just report what others thought about Him, but to also reveal who they thought that He was. Remember that one of Mark's constant themes was asking and answering the question of just "Who is this man, Jesus?" In order to answer the question, the disciples were required to publically commit themselves to their position on Jesus.

I think Jesus asked the question to force the disciples to really think about who they thought He was. Before Jesus could send them out to teach about Him, He had to be sure that the disciples fully understood exactly who He was. Incorrect teaching from the disciples about Jesus could damage Jesus' reputation and create a false impression about Jesus. If the disciples taught that Jesus was only a prophet, they had missed the entire point of Jesus' life and message. After all, God had sent many prophets that people killed without their death being sacrificial and redemptive. When Jesus sent the disciples out to preach in Mk 6:12, they only preached a message of repentance.

Peter, as the usual spokesperson for the disciples, waved his hand in the air and begged Jesus to call on him. I imagine Jesus taking a deep breath and saying, "OK, Peter. Who do you think I am?"[13] Peter correctly identified Jesus as the Christ. **Notice** that Peter didn't say "a christ", but "the Christ." This was an incredibly important title in the Jewish culture of the first century. Christ was the Greek word used to translate the Hebrew "messiach" or messiah. In Hebrew, the word literally meant, "to be anointed by God" or in common usage "to be picked by God to accomplish His purpose." Moses and David were "anointed" by God for His purpose, but so was Cyrus, a pagan ruler (Is 45:1). To the Jews, almost anyone could be "a" messiah as long as God chose him or her.

The first century Jews were desperately anticipating and looking for a messiah to deliver them from Rome. While their exact expectations differed, most of them were looking for an earthly leader who would kick out the Roman oppressors, restore Israel to its former borders and power and make the world bow down to Israel (and by the way to its God). The correct interpretation of this messiah title was crucial to Jesus' reputation and how the public reacted to Him. If Jesus were the publically accepted vision of Messiah or Christ, then the rebellion prone area of Galilee was primed to follow him in military action.

---

[13] *Any resemblance between Peter and Horschach on the old TV show "Welcome Back Cotter" is sacrilegious, spiritually immature and shows your age. Of course, now you know exactly what I was thinking about when I read the passage in Mark.*

This type of small, but violent uprising was fairly common in the first century, but was quickly crushed by the Romans. See Acts 21:37-38 for a more common first century rebellion. Rome stationed troops in Judea for this exact purpose. In fact, Herod became King in the time before Jesus by quelling revolt and enforcing peace under Roman rule in Judea. A successful revolt by the Hebrew Maccabee boys in 170 BC, which freed and restored Israel from its Egyptian oppressors, may have set the pattern for Jewish Messianic expectations in the first century.[14]

The disciples were at the crossroads in their relationship with Jesus. Before this in Mark, Jesus performed miracles and taught about the Kingdom of God (Mk 1-8:21). After this, Jesus turned to His disciples and in Mk 8: 31-38; 9: 31-32; and 10:32-34 taught them what it meant to be the Son of Man and what it really meant to be one of His disciples. Based on what Mark wrote, the disciples desperately needed both lessons. I suspect his audience then and today needs the same lessons.

In cultural terms, Peter attempted to assign a title to Jesus. Jesus rejected that title by telling Peter and the disciples not to call Him Messiah, but instead, the Son of Man. If Jesus had allowed Peter to assign Him the title of Messiah, Jesus would in effect have been agreeing with the title and everything that was popularly associated with that title. I think Jesus told the disciples not to use the title because they really didn't understand what it really meant to be "the Messiah."[15]

If they had spread their well meaning, but false, message about Jesus as the Messiah, people would have gotten the wrong idea and probably would have acted incorrectly based on those ideas. Remember Jesus said that His kingdom was not of this world (Jn 18:36). Jesus came to convert hearts and not to conquer the world militarily. Jesus was going to be the sacrificial Son of Man and not the world's idea of the messiah. Of course, this all changed after the resurrection and Pentecost, when the disciples received the Holy Spirit and were enlightened.

Jesus was willing to accept "The Son of Man" as a title and taught the disciples exactly what was involved in this different name. The Son of Man would not be the popular vision of a conquering messianic hero,

---

[14] Related to nothing, but an interesting historical note, one of the Maccabee boys was killed when an elephant sat on him.

[15] In the famous and often quoted words of Inigo Montoya from "The Princess Bride," "You keep using that word, I do not think it means what you think it means."

but would be the conquered servant who would sacrifice Himself for others.[16] The Son of Man would have His reputation ruined, be despised, tortured, killed and resurrected. As usual, the disciples just didn't get the message. While none of the disciples seemed to pick up on the resurrection prediction, they did understand that Jesus was predicting His own defamation and death.

Peter pulled Jesus out of the circle of amazed disciples and began to "rebuke" Jesus about this Suffering Son of Man stuff (Mk 8:32). The Greek word used here for rebuke indicated strong emotion and action and was the same word used to describe Jesus's exorcism of demons when He "rebuked" them. It always amazes me that the same Peter who just acknowledged Jesus as the Messiah had no problem fifteen seconds later taking this "Messiah" aside and "rebuking" Him in front of all the other disciples. I sometimes wonder if Peter had a filter between what he thought and said. It encourages me that with all his failings, Peter was still an accepted and eventually a successful disciple. Maybe there is a chance for you and me.

I think Peter's problem was that he couldn't get past his understanding of what it meant to be "the Messiah." If we put aside all our preconceived notions and years of Bible teaching we can probably understand Peter's problem. Remember that the public perception of the messiah in the first century was someone who was guaranteed to be successful because he was accomplishing God's purpose. Just like it had been impossible for Moses or David to die before they had accomplished God's purpose, it would be impossible for the first century Messiah to die before He had militarily restored Israel to its glory, status and position in the world.

I can just hear Peter say, "Jesus, you must be crazy. There is no way God's anointed one can be killed. You can't be that kind of Messiah. It just won't work out. What we need to do is get together with those zealots and get ready to attack some Romans. After all, God wants you to be a military hero like those Maccabee boys. If You just do what I tell You to do, You can't lose. Oh, and by the way, if You lose, that means I also lose everything."[17] Peter wanted Jesus to be the kind of Messiah that matched Peter's expectations and not God's true plan.

---

[16] *This new concept was a perfect match for the "suffering servant" or Messianic sections of Isaiah, but the disciples apparently were not ready to understand the connection (Is 52:13-53:12 and others).*

[17] *See Mk 10:28.*

Mark described Jesus' reaction to Peter's enthusiastic but completely misinformed coaching in his typically short and descriptive fashion. Jesus looked around, saw that He had the attention of the other disciples and publically "rebuked" Peter by calling him "Satan" (Mk 8:33). I guess that put Peter in his place. I also expect some of the other disciples chuckled at Peter being shamed by Jesus. After all, they probably got tired of Peter always being around the teacher and answering his questions. No one likes a "Teacher's Pet."[18] James and John illustrated this rivalry when they asked Jesus if they could sit on His right and left in His glory (Mk 10:35-37). Notice they didn't include a place for Peter.

I also expect that at least some of the other disciples probably shared Peter's opinion of Jesus as the Messiah. They needed the rebuke as much as Peter did. If Peter was the designated spokesman for the disciples, he was also the designated whipping boy. A teaching to Peter was a lesson to all the disciples. I wonder if we need the same lesson today?

Jesus explained that He called Peter Satan because Peter was tempting Him the same way Satan temped Him in the wilderness (Mt 4:10). Both Satan and Peter wanted Jesus to be their kind of messiah and not God's kind of Messiah. Now I think Peter was well meaning, but his confused understanding put him on Satan's side instead of God's side. Unknown to Peter, I think Satan used the popular conception of Messiah to once again tempt Jesus to depart from God's path. It was one thing to be tempted by Satan, who I assume Jesus knew was an opponent. It was another thing to be tempted by an enthusiastic and well-meaning friend and follower who only had "Your best interest at heart."[19]

After attempting to correct Peter and the disciples, Jesus called the crowd together and taught them all the same lesson about exactly who the Son of Man was going to be and what it meant to be a disciple of that Son of Man. Apparently it was a hard lesson because Mark showed Jesus teaching the same thing three times in this section (Mk 8: 31-38; 9: 31-32; and 10:32-34). By the way, everyone deserted Jesus before His arrest. No one understood who Jesus was until after His resurrection.

---

[18] *A modern example of how a title can carry a lot of social weight.*

[19] *Paul has the same problem in Acts 21:7-14, but he didn't call anyone Satan.*

MARK 8: *Jesus teaching how to be a disciple*

ACTIVITIES

Create a narrative outline of the chapter, a list of the characters and a list of the titles used in the chapter.

Questions for further discussion or reflection

1. Are we still looking for signs? Is our faith based on a continuous stream of miracles? How can we have read what we have read, seen what we have seen, and still not understand who Jesus is and what it means to follow Him?

2. Mk 8:18 is one of the few specific Old Testament references in Mark's Gospel and quotes Isaiah describing a generation who refused to listen to God's prophet. From the perspective of Mark's audience, would they make the same mistake? From our modern perspective will we make the same mistake?

3. Mark brought us to a strong climax in Mk 8:21 about the lack of understanding and then changed the theme and subject – or does he? The two-stage healing of the blind man was a strange miracle by any account. Was the healing so difficult that Jesus couldn't do it all at once? Why does Jesus ask the blind man if he can see after the first partial healing? Does the miracle have any connection to what just happened and what will happen in the next few chapters? Who is this Jesus and what does it mean to be His disciple?

4. Why do you think the chapter ends with Jesus talking about shame? Do you think that He thought the disciples were ashamed of Jesus as the "Son of Man?" Were they ashamed to be His disciples if He wasn't going to assume the title of Messiah? Were they ashamed that they had given their entire lives to someone who was going to be condemned and killed as a politically subversive deviant and criminal? Are we any different today? How do we shame Jesus with our actions or thoughts today? If you are ashamed of Jesus, will you lose your soul to the world? What does it mean in today's terms to not be ashamed of Jesus? How does a true disciple live today?

5. Do we have any confused ideas about Jesus today? What happens if we spread that false information around? We may think we have a good idea about sin, grace, redemption and salvation, but maybe we should go back to the Bible and make sure what we think is true actually matches what God says.

6. Read the Sermon on the Mount from Mt 5-7 and think about what it really means to be a member of the Kingdom of Heaven. Should you focus on making sure you look and are like a member in that kingdom before you go about "improving" anyone else? How can you change or what do you need to do the show your kingdom membership to the world?

7. You have probably read many books and heard many sermons about what it means to follow Jesus, but spend some time thinking about what it means to deny yourself. Think about it in these terms. What is your "self?" Is it your public image, your own sense of self, your sense of self-importance or might it be everything that you are? Are you ready to give up everything you are and put Christ first? If you gave up everything about yourself that was you and only kept the things that were Christ, would there be much left?

8. What kind of titles do we throw around today without thinking about the implications? Have you used some of them to describe yourself or others? What has been the positive or negative impact of this name calling? Would Jesus rebuke us about any titles we have used to describe Him?

9. Why does Jesus care about what people think? Isn't any publicity good publicity? What do you think Mark is trying to accomplish in this section?

The Gospel of Mark

Mark 9: *Jesus Teaching About God's Kingdom*

- You will see the Kingdom of God coming in power
- Transfiguration
- Disciples argue about what they saw
- The disciples have a "return to earth" experience
- Jesus predicts His death a second time and teaches about discipleship
- Jesus uses exaggeration for effect
- Devotion - The power of one
- Activities: Questions for further reflection

MARK 9

Jesus Teaching About God's Kingdom

The first part of Mark started with a vision of God announcing that Jesus was His Son. If you go back and read carefully, you will see that Mark did not show anyone other than Jesus hearing God's declaration. Right from the beginning, the original reader of Mark knew something that the characters in the Gospel didn't know. **Notice** that the second half started the same way and with similar words. The difference in the second half was that the three closest disciples were present. They saw and heard what God had to say. In the first section God addressed Jesus. In the second section God talked to the three disciples. Also **notice** that God told the disciples to listen to Jesus and not Moses or Elijah. *For whose benefit do you think the Transfiguration happened? What do you think this means to us today?*

Rather than repeating what you can read from a commentary, I am going to ask a lot of questions in this section. Remember that the disciples and Mark's audience probably had a lot of the same questions, but they didn't have a good commentary to turn to. Of course, they had a pretty good teacher to help them along the way. I hope and pray that as you reflect on and answer these questions that you will identify with the disciples and the original readers of Mark's Gospel. As always, look for your answers in the text itself.

Narratively, let's review what happens in the chapter and see how Mark's story speaks to us..

MARK 9: *Jesus Teaching About God's Kingdom*

Jesus Makes a Cryptic Statement About the Kingdom of God - Mk 9:1

What is He referring to – the Transfiguration, Crucifixion, Resurrection and Ascension, Pentecost or His second coming? What is the power of the kingdom of God?[20]

Does His statement refer forward to what will happen or is it a promise to encourage the disciples who have just been told what they must do to follow Jesus? Remember that Mark didn't write in chapter and verse. In the original Gospel, this passage immediately followed what preceded it without any chapter division. Is this another example of Mark showing us a Jesus prediction and then immediately showing its fulfillment? Doesn't the simple meaning of the context of the text indicate that what follows Mk 9:1 is a fulfillment of the power of the Kingdom of God? When was Jesus' real victory over Satan? Does this change how you understand and apply the sequence of events in this chapter?

Transfiguration - Mk 9:2-8

Why six days later (Ex 24:16)? Why a mountaintop? Is there another Old Testament connection? Why does God speak out of a cloud? (One more Old Testament connection?) Why Moses and Elijah? Was this yet another Old Testament connection? (Hint - Moses and Elijah were the premier figures in the Hebrew Old Testament.) Moses represented the law and Elijah represented the prophets. **Notice** *that God tells the disciples to listen to Jesus and not Moses or Elijah. Is God strongly reminding the disciples that Jesus is His Son and the Christ even if He has to go to Jerusalem and die?*[21]

The Disciples Argue About What they Saw - Mk 9:9-13

Does anything about the disciples' reaction remind you of Nicodemus? Did they get tangled up in a theological argument that made them completely miss Jesus' point? Why did Jesus tell them not to discuss what happened

---

[20] Everyone already knew what the power of the Roman Empire was. It was the power to intimidate, oppress, enslave and, if necessary, kill. A person could exist in the Roman Empire, but only by accommodating everything in his or her life to the Emperor. For instance, you had to worship Caesar as a god. If you didn't, you were unpatriotic as well as being an "atheist."

[21] The Greek word translated as transformed is metamorphe. See Rom 12:1; 2 Cor 3:18 and Matt 17:2. Why doesn't Mark tell us what Moses and Elijah were saying to Jesus? I wonder what else Mark knew that he didn't record in his Gospel?

until after His resurrection?[22] *Having seen and heard, are they still blind? They obviously know what they saw, but what did it mean? Does anyone see a parallel to the dual stage healing of the blind man? He saw (understood) things dimly or in outline, but didn't really see them well. How well did the disciples see at this point? Were they really ready to spread the good news about Jesus? Did they even really understand who He was and what His kingdom would be like? Do we suffer the same problem today?*

The Disciples Return to Earth from a "Mountaintop Experience" and Face the Reality of Their Failure to Heal the Epileptic Boy - Mk 9:14-39

Why aren't the disciples able to heal the boy? Where does the disciples' power come from? How do they access that power? Does this have anything to do with their common topic of conversation? Read Mk 8:32, 9:33 and 10:37. Do the disciples understand what the power of the Kingdom of God was really like? Notice *that someone "tells" the disciples what to do in Mk 9:18. What did that say about the father's vision of the Kingdom of God? Was the father trying to control God by "telling" Him what to do? Is this the right way to approach the Kingdom of God?*

When and how does the father show faith? How was the father's request of Jesus in Mk 9:22, 24 different from the command to the disciples? Is the difference significant? (Hint – anytime a professor, pastor or author asks a question like that, the answer is probably yes.) Does Jesus answer all prayers and requests? (See Mk 10:35-40.) Is the problem what Jesus can do or what the father needs to do? What does this mean for us today? Does Jesus demand perfect belief and faith? What does this passage tell us about the Kingdom of God? (See, this is another one of those questions that almost certainly requires a yes as the answer. 😊 *)*

Read Heb 11:1-6 and Eph 2:8-9. *Where does our faith come from? What do we need to do to get it? Is our prayer any different from the father's prayer to Jesus? How many of the heroes of the faith mentioned in Heb 11 died before they saw the fulfillment of God's promise? Did Abraham ever see his descendants outnumber the stars or the sand on the beach? Is the real meaning of faith to believe in God's ability to provide and answer His promises even if we don't see their immediate fulfillment?*

---

[22] *This concept of concealment is generally known as the Messianic Secret and appears all through Mark.*

MARK 9: *Jesus Teaching About God's Kingdom*

Jesus Predicts His Death a Second Time - Mk 9:30-32

Notice how closely this followed the pattern of Mk 8:31. Mark must really be trying to make a point here. Given the limited amount of space he had in which to write, anything Mark repeated must have been important. Also **notice** that the disciples still didn't get it.[23] Instead of getting mad, Jesus treated this as another teaching opportunity and used a child for an acted out parable. In Jewish and Roman culture, a child was the least and most insignificant being in the household. Slaves might well have more status than a young child. *When we lead our daily lives, do we deal with the least and most insignificant or do we deal with the important and powerful? Do we do what we think is important or do we do what God thinks is important? Where does our power as Christians come from? How do we use that power? Do we try to do things under our own power or depend on prayer for guidance?*

Jesus Uses Exaggeration for Effect - Mk 9:42-50

Some people believe that you must follow each word of the Bible based on its literal meaning. These people have a problem with this section. Is Jesus really saying for us to pluck out an eye or cut off a hand? In other places, Jesus tells us that we can sin just by looking at something and thinking about it. (Mt 6) Based on that, there should be a whole lot of one-eyed Christians running around with just one hand.[24]

I think that the Bible needs to be understood literally, but it also needs to be interpreted intelligently. Hebrew culture commonly used exaggeration for effect. To me, this section is a pretty clear case of Jesus trying to make a point by exaggerating. *Do you see Jesus exaggerating for effect in any of the other Gospels? You don't have to agree with me. What do you think is the point of this passage?*

I can't take credit for the following devotion. My wife, Emma, wrote it. I think it speaks to this situation and is a good example of how you can explain the Biblical text and call for action today based on the text.

---

[23] *Can you imagine how patient Jesus must have been? Do you think He ever wanted to call down a few thunderbolts to "discipline" a few of the "disciples?"*

[24] *Of course I am exaggerating for effect. I wonder if anyone else ever did that?*

MARK 9: *Jesus Teaching About God's Kingdom*

The synagogue in Capernaum – just across from Peter's house. The current ruins are rebuilt on the same foundation as the first century synagogue, so they show us how large Peter's synagogue really was.

MARK 9: *Jesus Teaching About God's Kingdom*

People still stand on the stones as they talk and lecture to the crowds.

MARK 9: *Jesus Teaching About God's Kingdom*

The Power of One. The Power of Simple Things in Sharing the Gospel (Mk 9:33-50)

Standing in the synagogue at Capernaum looking out over the Sea of Galilee, I can imagine Jesus teaching from the sacred scrolls or maybe without any notes since, after all, He is the Word. These synagogue remains are where Peter and the others from this seaside village would gather, walking across the street from their houses, to hear the Great Teacher. In teaching, Jesus would look around Him and use everyday objects and tasks to reveal Himself to the working men and women of His day. Jesus wanted His followers to have hearts as well as heads full of Scripture. He used concrete examples that His audience could immediately understand and apply.

Millstones in Capernaum under construction and on display.

The synagogue is awe inspiring and Peter's house a stone's throw from the synagogue makes Peter somehow more like me, an everyday citizen with a house and a job. It is the many millstones and olive and grape presses scattered in the yard beside the synagogue that speak to me. Capernaum was not only an important fishing village; it was also the site for millstone manufacturing, with the businesses putting their inventory out in the open for public display. After all, rain won't hurt a rock. I can see Jesus teaching, perched on a millstone perhaps not quite ready for the grain merchant who had ordered it. Perhaps with a piece of bread in His hand (since I am sure they had lunch on the synagogue lawn just like we do), Jesus continues the message He had started earlier in the synagogue. "Who is the greatest in the Kingdom of Heaven?" (Mt. 18:1; Mk 9:34)

MARK 9: *Jesus Teaching About God's Kingdom*

His point is that there is no rank in His kingdom. This is as much an alien idea to these men and women who know their rank and status in the village society and in the Roman Empire as it is to us who live in the 21st century world. Each has his or her own rank depending on the societal structure being used as the measure. But all of those measures are of the world and not of His kingdom. He casts His eyes around for something to help make His point, something His audience can identify with.

Jesus points to the other millstones around Him or even the one He is standing on. Maybe others are seated on some of the stones like He is. They have all pretty much ignored their surroundings. They are here to hear the Teacher. Now the message becomes real. Jesus calls one of the children seated nearby with his family to come sit on His knee for a minute. Then Jesus says, "Truly unless you are converted and become like children, you shall not enter the Kingdom of Heaven... whoever causes one of these little ones [and He waves His hand out to the other children who have begun to squirm their way closer to this Teacher who is gentle and caring for their little peer] who believe in Me to stumble, it is better for him [and here Jesus points to the stone upon which He is seated and the others around Him] that a heavy millstone be hung around his neck, and that he be drowned in the depth of the sea." (Mt. 18:3-7; Mk 9:42)

Can't you almost hear the parents suck in a big breath wondering at the harshness of Jesus' statement and wondering what their innocent little children will now think of the gentle Teacher? But Jesus has only begun to shock His audience. He continues to talk of the stumbling blocks of the world - big huge stumbling blocks like these millstones that a single man can barely move without help. And yet, when the stone is removed from this yard and put into service, it helps feed hundreds or thousands of hungry people. One stone removed. One person doing his simple job of making a stone to grind the farmer's wheat so many can eat. One lowly stone cutter helping one lowly farmer or grain merchant so many average families can eat and, in turn, do their daily work and raise their children.

Jesus turns back to the child on His knee and those seated around Him and continues speaking to the parents. "See that you do not despise one of these little ones, for I say to you, that their angels in heaven continually behold the face of My Father who is in Heaven. For the Son of Man has come to save that which was lost." (Mt. 18:10-11) Then Jesus looks away from the Sea and back over His shoulders to the green pastures of the Galilean hills beyond His audience and tells the story of the shepherd who seeks his one lost sheep while the other ninety-nine are safely in the pen. (Mt. 18:12) Jesus is there, and here today, to save each person.

No one has rank over another. We are all His precious children made in His image. Jesus came for each of us and He shows us that by using everything around us in our daily lives to show us His love and His desperate desire to see all of His creations returned to Him for eternity. Jesus tells a great story, but He also demonstrates how we can indeed move stumbling blocks and even mountains by following His example.

The millstones of Capernaum remind me that Jesus' kingdom is won by one person at a time making the Gospel relevant to one another in his or her sphere of influence. What are you sitting on, wearing, or doing each day that could be used to share the Gospel? Are those "things" tools in your arsenal or stumbling blocks for sharing the Gospel? Take a moment to look around you and take an assessment. You are far better armed than you think. Peter reminds us that we must "always be ready to make a defense to everyone who asks you to give an account for the hope that is in you." (1 Pet 3:15) Jesus shows us how easy it is. There is no time like now to begin.

MARK 9: *Jesus Teaching About God's Kingdom*

ACTIVITIES

Create a narrative outline of the chapter, a list of the characters and a list of the titles used in the chapter.

Questions for further discussion or reflection

1. What is Jesus referring to in Mk 9:1 – the Transfiguration, Resurrection and Ascension, Pentecost or His second coming? What is the power of the kingdom of God? Does His statement refer forward to what will happen or is it a promise to encourage the disciples who have just been told what they must do to follow Jesus? Doesn't the simple meaning of the context of the text indicate that what follows Mk 9:1 is a fulfillment of the power of the Kingdom of God? When was Jesus' real victory over Satan? Does this change how you understand and apply the sequence of events in this chapter?

2. Why did Mark make the point about the transfiguration happening six days later? (Ex 24:16). Why a mountaintop? Is there another Old Testament connection? Why does God speak out of a cloud? (One more Old Testament connection?) Why Moses and Elijah? Was this yet another Old Testament connection? (Hint - Moses and Elijah were the premier figures in the Hebrew Old Testament.) Moses represented the law and Elijah represented the prophets. Is God strongly reminding the disciples that Jesus is His Son and the Christ even if He has to go to Jerusalem and die?

3. When and how does the father show faith? How was the father's request of Jesus in Mk 9:22, 24 different from the command to the disciples? Is the difference significant?

4. Does Jesus answer all prayers and requests? (See Mk 10:35-40.) Is the problem what Jesus can do or what the father needs to do? What does this mean for us today? Does Jesus demand perfect belief and faith? What does this passage tell us about the Kingdom of God?

5. When we lead our daily lives, do we deal with the least and most insignificant or do we deal with the important and powerful? Do we do what we think is important or do we do what God thinks is important? Where does our power as Christians come from? How do we use that power? Do we try to do things under our own power or depend on prayer for guidance?

The Gospel of Mark

Mark 10: *Jesus Teaches Again on How to Be a Disciple*

- How do you enter the Kingdom of God?
- Teaching about discipleship on the road to Jerusalem
- The healing of blind Bartimaeus
- The path of true discipleship is the road to Jerusalem and the way of the cross
- Activities: Questions for further reflection

MARK 10

More Teaching on Discipleship

Notice how this chapter ends with Jesus healing a blind man. Does that remind you of anything else? (Mk 8:22) Many people think these two healings are book ends for this section of Mark. Chapters 8-10 all deal with Jesus teaching His disciples while they are "on the way" to Jerusalem. The phrase "on the way" is very important for Mark.[25] **Notice** that these three chapters are joined together as a segment. After this the miracles cease, Jesus enters Jerusalem, and the action level really picks up. These three chapters are the calm before the storm and deal with Jesus teaching His disciples about what it means to follow Jesus. The passage ends with what I think is an example of how a real disciple reacts to Jesus. (Mk 10:46-52)

With that as an introduction, here is a brief narrative outline for this chapter.

> Jesus engages in a discussion about divorce with the Pharisees.
>
> Jesus teaches about children.
>
> Jesus talks to a rich young man who says he wants to inherit eternal life.
>
> Jesus repeats His teaching about what will happen to Him and how His disciples should lead. This is the third time Jesus has reacted to the lack of understanding about what it means to be a disciple by strongly teaching His disciples (Mk 8:31; 9:31; 10:32). Do you see a pattern?
>
> Jesus heals Blind Bart.

---

[25] *See the discussion on Mk 10:32-45 for a fuller discussion of this topic.*

MARK 10: *Jesus teaches again on how to be a disciple*

From a narrative or story point of view, you should ask yourself why Mark put these events together here. If you read the text carefully, there is nothing that demands the events take place in sequential and chronological order. I believe that while Mark accurately recorded true events in the life of Jesus, he did not necessarily record them in the order in which they took place.[26] If this is true, there must be some reason Mark put these stories together in this sequence and put them at this place in his Gospel.

How Do You Enter the Kingdom of God? - Mk 10: 13-31

What do we have to do to inherit eternal life? (Mk 10:15) In this passage, Jesus taught on how you entered His Kingdom. From a worldly perspective, you entered a kingdom by status – either status you were born with (being born to Roman citizens) or you bought your way into status with a great deal of money (buying Roman citizenship). The more important you were in the world, the more likely you were to be a member of the important (Roman) kingdom. The followers of Christ needed to learn that membership in God's Kingdom was not something a person could buy, deserve by high status or birth.

Why can the rich young man not get what he wants? What does he really want most in life? What was Jesus' reaction to the rich man? Notice that the young man quotes a bunch of the Ten Commandments. We naturally assume that he is following all of them. If you closely examine the text you will discover that the young man leaves out several significant commandments - particularly the one about coveting. Jesus nails it when He tells the young man to sell everything in order to enter into eternal life. Based on the young man's reaction, his love of wealth will keep him from eternal life. In the time of Jesus, Jews believed that God blessed people by making them rich. The rich were blessed for their righteousness and the poor were being punished by poverty. Think about the example of Job. When he was wealthy, everyone thought he had a great relationship with God. When things went badly for Job, everyone thought that some kind of secret sin in his life caused God to be mad with him.

What the disciples are really saying is, "If a rich man (who is obviously being favored by God) can't get into heaven, what chance do we have?"

---

[26] *Most scholars agree with me here. Even if I am wrong and Mark is being accurate chronologically and sequentially, he still picked what to present and what to leave out. Obviously much must have happened between His teaching in Capernaum (Mk 9) and his arrival in Jerusalem (Mk 11). You still have to ask, "Why did Mark present these events in this sequence?"*

Notice that Peter makes a point of telling Jesus that they abandoned everything (perhaps gave up God's material blessing) in order to follow Him. Would they ever see any of their blessings again? Also notice that another teaching on discipleship immediately follows the disciples' lack of understanding about earthly and heavenly power and blessings. Jesus reassured them that the only way into God's Kingdom was not by human status or means but by God's power.

In Mk 10:35, John and James showed that either they weren't listening to Jesus' teaching or that they didn't take Him seriously. They don't demand that Jesus do what they want (like the father of the epileptic boy), but they do say they want Him to do what they "ask." Remember that Jesus had just predicted His own degradation and death. The Sons of Thunder's only concern is that they be closest to Jesus in His glory! Have I mentioned recently how patient Jesus was? Notice that Jesus asked them the same question He will ask Blind Bartimaeus in Mk 10:51. *Do you think these two stories were related? Which person showed the real attitude of a disciple? Do you think Mark may have used these two stories as an example of a misguided disciple (Sons of Thunder) and an example of a good disciple (Blind Bartimaeus)?*

Teaching About Discipleship on The Way to Jerusalem - Mk 10:31-45

This is the last and most intense of three times that Jesus tried to teach His disciples what it really meant to be His follower. Each Jesus teaching episode (Mk 8:31-38; 9:31-40 and 10:32-45) concluded with Mark recording the disciples acting in a way that proved they had absolutely no understanding of what Jesus had just taught. Jesus tried to teach them the Kingdom of God's method of discipleship, but they remained stuck with the world's conception of what it meant to be a servant.

As an aside, the way Mark portrayed the disciples is one indication that he didn't just make up all the things he wrote down. Given that Mark knew Peter and presumably had a relatively high opinion of Peter and the other disciples (otherwise, why take time to write about them?), why would Mark show them being so uncomprehending and uncaring unless they really were that dense. Three times Jesus told them that He was getting ready to be killed and their only response was to argue with Him (Mk 8:32; 9:34; 10:35) about their own personal issues. *On the other hand, are we any different today? Do we ever approach God and ask Him, "God, we want You to do for us whatever we ask of You" (Mk 10:35)?*

MARK 10: *Jesus teaches again on how to be a disciple*

Just as this is the most detailed description of what was going to happen to Jesus in Jerusalem, it is also the most blatant misunderstanding on the part of the disciples. John and James (the Sons of Thunder) come to Jesus and ask Him to give them a blank check. If I could paraphrase, they are asking Jesus to make them His right hand men with all of His authority and power. Not too shy, are they? Even worse, they apparently do this in front of the other ten disciples. I wonder how Peter and the others felt about that?

In defense of James and John, what they did was culturally appropriate from a worldly point of view. In any group or family structure, the men would be in a constant struggle for power, authority and status. They would always be measuring themselves against each other, jockeying to be closest to Jesus or trying to gain a small edge on one another. I don't want to be sacrilegious about this, but think about almost any gangster movie or political intrigue movie you have seen. From a worldly perspective, life was, and is, a cutthroat battle.

The three main disciples in Mark's Gospel were Peter, James and John. They accompanied Jesus at the Transfiguration and other critical times. James and John had just seen Peter rebuked by Jesus and they may have thought there was a power vacuum that they could fill. From their perspective, the only way to gain power was to take it from someone else. They correctly saw Jesus as the true source of power and authority and they were asking Him to do the worldly thing and distribute some of that power to them. After all, Peter had screwed up big time and James and John thought they were the perfect replacements. In Matthew, they even get their Momma to help them ask Jesus for power (Mt 20:20-21).

I can only imagine the patience Jesus had with His disciples. Rather than striking the Sons of Thunder with His own lightning, Jesus taught them once again what it really meant to be a disciple. First, He explained to them that they really didn't know what they are asking for. From our modern perspective and the perspective of Mark's audience in 60AD, we know what it would mean to be with Jesus in His glory.[27] In worldly terms, it meant a painful death. Jesus warns them that eventually they will share His fate, but apparently James and John couldn't really understand what that meant.

---

[27] *The Gospel of John makes it clear that the glorification of Jesus takes place at the crucifixion. What the world meant for the worst, God used for the best in redeeming all of creation.*

After Jesus' death James, John and Peter didn't struggle for leadership over the Jerusalem church. From what we can tell from the Gospels, leadership went to a different James, the brother of Jesus, who didn't even believe in or support Jesus during His earthly ministry. Discussing that change from enemy to leader is another book, but Jesus did the same thing with Saul/Paul on the Damascus Road.

Mark ended this passage with Jesus once more teaching what it really meant to be His disciple. Rather than the worldly way of the Gentiles lording it over people, a disciple of Jesus would be a servant for others.

The implication was that the bigger leader you wanted to be, the more you had to be a servant. If you wanted to be first in line, you had to be willing to be last. Jesus used Himself as an example of someone who came to serve rather than be served. Nothing about being a disciple matched the standards of earthly glory and as much as the disciples wanted the earthly glory, they would be last in the Kingdom of Heaven.

There are several lessons we can learn from this passage. The first is that sometimes the answer to prayer is, "No!" and the negative answer is really for our benefit. Jesus flat refused the request of James and John, although He did warn them that they would eventually share in His "glory." James and John didn't really know what they were asking and Jesus, in His greater wisdom, refused to let them die with Him. He had other plans for them. Second, the places by Jesus in His glory were not His to assign. In this world, Jesus was constantly obedient to God, His Father. God had already determined that Jesus would be crucified between two criminals as His right and left companions. Being executed among criminals would be the final insult the world could deliver. That death in service to God would be the very thing that God would use to redeem mankind and all of creation. God has a habit of taking the evil of the world and using it to accomplish His own purpose.[28]

The final point was that Jesus was willing to follow God's path or way to offer Himself as a sacrifice in order to redeem or ransom the many. That is the pattern that Jesus wanted the disciples to follow. Jesus was on "the way" to Jerusalem and death and He wanted His disciples to "follow Him on the way." The following passage with Blind Bartimeus drove this message home one final time. The ultimate path of a disciple is to "follow Jesus on the way" of God's path wherever that might lead, even to a sacrificial death.

---

[28] *This is not just a New Testament concept. Go back and read Gn 50:20.*

MARK 10: *Jesus teaches again on how to be a disciple*

Titles Given to and Accepted by Jesus: The Healing of Blind Bartimaeus - Mk 10:46-52

Make a list of everything the blind man does that illustrates true discipleship. Be ready to discuss this passage with others in your group. Pay attention to what the text says. Here are some hints. *Does Mark normally name the people who are healed? Why do you think Bart is named? What does he call Jesus? Why is this important? (Is 11:1-3, the line of Jesse refers to David's descendants.) How did he react when people told him to shut up? What did he ask for? What did he need? What was the common view of blind people in the time of Jesus? How did Jesus react to the request? Remember that Jesus knows that He is walking to His death in Jerusalem. If you were in Jesus' shoes, what would your attitude be? Would you pay attention to some beggar calling your name from the side of the road? Is there a sermon here?*

What did Jesus give him? Why did Jesus do it? How did Bart react when Jesus called him? Why does Mark mention Bart's cloak? How did Bart address Jesus? How was this different from the way the rich young man addressed Jesus? How did Bart react to his healing? Right after this, Jesus gets into a serious conflict with the religious leaders in Jerusalem. Isn't it interesting that a blind man understands who Jesus is and what He can do, but the religious leadership (who should be leading all the people in righteousness) totally misses Jesus?

The Path to True Discipleship Is the Road to Jerusalem and the Way of the Cross - Mk 10:52

This is our closing bookend of healing blind people and it matches the two-stage healing of the blind person in Bethsaida (Mk 8:22). **Notice** the focus on discipleship. Mark ends the passage with the key phrase describing Bartimaeus "following Jesus on the way." In Mark this is the

MARK 10: *Jesus teaches again on how to be a disciple*

language of discipleship. In effect, Blind Bart has become a disciple. *Is Bartimaeus Mark's example of what a disciple should be and a role model for the other "partially blind" disciples?* This passage acts as a "hinge" by closing off the teaching on discipleship and introducing the Jerusalem Passion section of Mark's Gospel.

What follows is a section from my dissertation on Mark. Please excuse the footnotes and academic language. I think it makes some good points about Bartimaeus, hopefully without getting too dry and boring.

> Examine the titles or names that Bartimaeus used and that Jesus allowed Bartimaeus to use. Remembering Jesus' encounter with Peter, Jesus had no trouble publicly rebuking Peter when he tried to get Jesus to accept the wrong name or the context associated with that name. Jesus accepted from Bartimaeus the titles of Rabonni and Son of David. Other people clearly heard him use these titles because they told him to be quiet. Even though he was blind, Bartimaeus didn't allow anything to stop him from getting to Jesus.
>
> Bartimaeus was the first person that Mark showed publicly identifying Jesus with the theologically loaded title, Son of David. The implications attached to the name Son of David were similar to those associated with the Son of Man title. The title could be a literal description of any son of a father named David, or the name could be a claim to the line of the Davidic kingship with status high enough to rule over all Israel. Jesus' acceptance of this title without contradiction from the crowd was consistent with behaviors in the first century. If a person truly had the characteristic described, the appropriate response would be to accept the crowd's acclaim. In the crowd's opinion, a title like the Son of David fit Jesus because his actions warranted such accolades and honors. By allowing someone like Bartimaeus to name Jesus as the Son of David, the crowd was in essence accepting Jesus as a legitimate son of David. **Notice** that the crowd's acceptance and naming continued as Jesus enters Jerusalem (Mt 21:9). The people leave town to greet Jesus and welcome Him to Jerusalem. Normally, this was the way visiting monarchs were greeted.

Bartimaeus's use of the label Son of David was the only time Mark applied that name to Jesus and was the first of the triumphal titles assigned to Jesus as He prepared to enter Jerusalem. France thought that the title was, without a doubt, messianic. "For Jewish people it would be functionally equivalent to Christ, but the voicing of David's name increases the loading of royal and nationalistic ideology which it carries."[29] Lane thought that the name was used as flattery to attract Jesus' attention, since Bartimaeus did not use the title when he directly conversed with Jesus.[30] Even if Bartimaeus did not mean the title as a messianic reference, Jesus publicly accepted the title. In this case, the acceptance of the title that the common person would have heard as messianic was more important than exactly how Bartimaeus meant the title to be used.[31]

At this point in Mark, clearly the titles for Jesus of demon-inspired exorcist and Sabbath-breaking blasphemer had not won much public acceptance. The Pharisees and Herodians had not gained the necessary public support for their efforts to label Jesus as a deviant. On the other hand, Jesus' actions in Jerusalem and the Temple caused conflict with a more powerful interest group. The Jerusalem power structure would demonstrate that they had successfully named Jesus as a deviant by forcing him to endure arrest, public humiliation, beatings, and crucifixion.

The gloves were getting ready to come off for the final confrontation in Jerusalem. Jesus' true names and nature would be revealed to everyone and His glory would be displayed to the world. Unfortunately the crowds welcoming Him to town found that Jesus was not the kind of Messiah they were expecting and His Kingdom was not going to throw the Romans out of Palestine.

---

[29] Evans pointed out that the title *Son of David* was in the initial or emphatic position in the Greek text, even though the name *Jesus* appears first in the English language text (Mark 10:47). Evans, 130 and France, 423.

[30] Boring pointed out that the Son of David was expected to come from Bethlehem and not Nazareth. Boring, 134 and Lane, 388.

[31] E. Lohse, "Uios Dauid," *TDNT* 8.482-92.

The crowd's acceptance of Jesus as the Son of David may be the first indication that the populace was gaining the correct consensus about Jesus. If true, the crowd's acceptance of Jesus was also very dangerous. The religious and political authorities could accept a healer coming to town or an unsupported madman who claimed to be the Messiah, but they could not afford to be challenged by a well-supported miracle worker who claimed divine prerogatives. Jesus' threat caused an immediate and staunch response from the Jewish priesthood. The Jewish leaders claimed that Jesus was a danger to the Jewish religion and the Roman civil authority. The final and successful charge against Jesus was that he was claiming to be King of the Jews and in rebellion against Caesar. Rome and Pilate could not ignore this political charge.

The final title used in the passage was Bartimaeus calling Jesus Rabbi. Only the disciples used the title Rabbi, or teacher, to address Jesus in Mark's Gospel (Mark 9:5; 12:21; 14:45).[32] Clearly, the term is one of respect. More importantly for Mark's narrative, Jesus allowed Bartimaeus to address him the same way the disciples addressed him.[33]

Jesus' acceptance of the title of "Rabboni" from Bartimaeus may mean that Jesus accepted him as a student or follower rather than a member of the crowd. The only people in Mark who called Jesus Rabbi are Peter, Judas, and Bartimaeus. None of Jesus' enemies or attackers used the title. Since the only followers of Jesus who are named in the Gospel are the disciples, Mark's use of Bartimaeus' name may be another indication that Bartimaeus became part of the in-group of disciples.

Just as Bartimaeus's physical blindness echoed the disciples' spiritual blindness, Jesus' question to Bartimaeus echoed his question to James and John (Mark 10:36). A blind man comprehended Jesus' identity as Messiah while the sighted disciples argued about

---

[32] *Mary Magdalene's reference to the risen Lord as rJabbouniv in John 20:16 is the only other New Testament usage of the term for Jesus.*

[33] *France, 424.*

who would sit at his right hand. A beggar beside the road demonstrated a level of comprehension that the disciples had not.[34] Bartimaeus' use of the term Rabboni indicated that approaching Jesus with an attitude of faith and respect were the marks of a disciple. Bartimaeus was ready and willing to leave everything behind in him commitment to follow Jesus "on the way." Bartimaeus' faith resulted in healing, and he assumed the role of a disciple when he followed Jesus on the way.[35]

Jesus made no attempt to control or quiet the crowd, a feature consistent with the cultural norms of the first century. When someone publicly performed an honorable action endorsed by the court of public opinion, the person gained status. The crowd spread the news to a wider audience, confirming the claim to honor. In this case, the actions of Jesus exactly matched behaviors that would be expected based on cultural norms. Maybe the crowd finally perceived the true nature of Jesus and His Kingdom.[36]

---

[34] "What Bartimaeus lacks in eyesight, he makes up for in insight." Edwards, 329.

[35] Witherington compared the new disciple with the previous disciples who thought they deserved a seat of honor. France, 425 and Witherington, 292.

[36] John H. Morris, *Concealment or Revelation: The Messianic Secret in Mark.* (Logos Publishing, 2013).

MARK 10: *Jesus teaches again on how to be a disciple*

ACTIVITIES

Create a narrative outline of the chapter, a list of the characters and a list of the titles used in the chapter.

Questions for further discussion or reflection

1. Why do you think Mark put the healing of blind people at the beginning and ending of Jesus' teaching on discipleship? What does this mean to you today?

2. What was Jesus' reaction to the rich young man? Why can the man not get what he wanted? Does the man want eternal life or something else?

3. Do you think the stories about Blind Bartimaeus and the Sons of Thunder are related? Do you think Mark put them close together in his Gospel for a purpose? What do you think that purpose was?

4. Make a list of everything the blind man does that illustrates true discipleship. Does Mark normally name the people who are healed? Why do you think Bart is named? What does he call Jesus? Why is this important? (Is 11:1-3, the line of Jesse refers to David's descendants.) How did he react when people told him to shut up? What did he ask for? What did he need? What was the common view of blind people in the time of Jesus? How did Jesus react to the request? Remember that Jesus knows that He is walking to His death in Jerusalem. If you were in Jesus' shoes, what would your attitude be? Would you pay attention to some beggar calling your name from the side of the road?

5. What did Jesus give him? Why did Jesus do it? How did Bart react when Jesus called him? Why does Mark mention Bart's cloak? How did Bart address Jesus? How was this different than the way the rich young man addressed Jesus?

6. How does our society influence our feelings about ourselves as better or worse in relationship to others? How do you think reality TV and the internet supports this process of comparison? What can we do to guard against this danger?

The Gospel of Mark

Mark 11: *Jesus Enters Jerusalem*

- Pictures of Jerusalem and the Temple
- The conquering King enters town on a donkey
- Parable of the fig tree and cleansing the Temple
- Mountain-moving faith
- Let the confrontation begin
- Activities: Questions for further reflection

MARK 11

Jesus Enters Jerusalem

Jerusalem and the Temple

This is a modern day model of the first century Temple. You can start to get an idea of how big the Temple complex was and how it completely dominated the Jerusalem city environment. You are looking at the main entrances to the Temple and the Southern steps where Jesus sat to teach His disciples. You can see the Antonio Fortress, where the Roman garrison was stationed, immediately behind and to the left of the Temple complex. Note that the tower of the Antonio fortress is high enough for the Romans to see down into the Temple complex. This was important because the crowds gathering in the Temple for Passover or some other ceremony tended to be emotionally charged and easy to incite to riot. Remember that the Romans saved Paul from a lynch mob in the Temple (Acts 21:27-36).

Herod rebuilt the Temple between the tops of two mountains in Jerusalem. To make a platform large enough to build on, he had the tops of the two mountains cut off and leveled. He used the material from the mountaintops to fill in the valley between the mountains and then built a platform on the created level space. On top of that platform, he built the Temple. This gives a new interpretation to having enough faith to move mountains, doesn't it?

To help put things in perspective, this is a modern picture of the "Wailing Wall" or "Western Wall" of the Temple. As massive as it is, this is not a wall of the Temple because the Romans completely destroyed the Temple in 70AD. What remains today is just the retaining wall Herod built to support the foundation of the Temple. The Temple stood on top of the wall you are looking at.

One last geeky picture because I just can't resist. This is a picture of part of one of the foundation stones at the bottom of the foundation wall. The entire stone is over 30 feet long.

What are the three major events that happen in this chapter? How do these events fit into what Jesus has been saying about His time in Jerusalem? What is the significance of Jesus riding in on a donkey over palm fronds and people's clothes? Where does the quote in verse 9 come from? Read Ps 118:22-29. What is the significance of this quote? Who did the people think Jesus was? Hosanna was a theologically loaded term. It literally meant "Lord Save Us!" To say something like that to a person was like a big brass band playing "Hail to the Chief." If you heard the tune, you expected to see the president. *What was the first thing Jesus did once he came to town? Where would you expect God's Son to go when He came to town?*

Remember how sacred the Temple was to the Jews. They believed that God literally lived in the Temple's Holy of Holies. Remember back in the Old Testament that God took up residence in the Temple. The people actually saw the glory of God coming into the Temple. Today, if you were to tour the Governor's mansion, it would not surprise you to see the Governor. When people went to the Temple, they were going to God's house and were expected to act appropriately. *How would you act if you were going to be within a few hundred feet of where God Himself "lived?" Would you dress up and make sure you were ritually clean? How would you feel if you entered the Governor's mansion and criminals were running an identify theft ring and a meth lab in the lobby? Would it make you wonder about the Governor and the government he represented? Would you be just a little aggravated about what they had done to your father's house?*

The Conquering King Enters Town on a Donkey - Mk 11:1- 10

This was not the most impressive way to enter town, but it did fulfill an Old Testament prophecy. More importantly, it indicated what kind of King and Messiah Jesus was and it showed that His Kingdom was much different from the Roman kingdom with its cohorts of military troops.

Did Jesus steal the donkey? Why do you think He did or did not? Was there anything significant about the donkey? Read Mk 14:13-16 when Jesus again sent out His disciples. Do you see any similarity? How did Jesus know about the room and the donkey? Was it Divine knowledge or did He have some secret disciples in the city? This is another example of where Mark didn't tell us everything he knew. If you read Acts, you may find a clue about Jesus' supporters in Jerusalem.

Since Jerusalem was a backwater town without proper "Roman" facilities, Pilate came to Jerusalem for Passover and left as soon as he could after Passover was complete. The only reason he came to town was in order to keep the peace during a time of increased potential for riot and revolt during Passover. He would have stayed out of town as long as possible and may well have entered Jerusalem on the Friday before Passover. If this is possible, Pilate may have entered from the North as the publicly accepted "King" of Jerusalem at the same time that Jesus entered from the East as the real King of Jerusalem. While this can't be proved, the concept is possible. Regardless, I think the comparison between the military pomp and glory of the Roman parade and God's Son humbly entering His city is a great picture of the difference between God's Kingdom and Caesar's Kingdom.

Parable of the Fig Tree and Cleaning of the Temple - Mk 11:11-22

Notice that we have a classic Markan "sandwich" here. We get the first part of the fig tree story, the Temple cleansing, and then the last part of the fig tree story. Many people think Mark did this on purpose. The first and third part help interpret the middle part or else the middle part helps interpret the first and third. I believe verses 13-21 must be interpreted together. Understanding one part helps you understand the others.

Why did Jesus say that He was cleaning the Temple? Remember this was His Father's house. What was going on in the Temple? Why was this bad? What was expected to go on in the Temple? What was one of God's first purposes in taking the Jews as His own people? The answer is that God wanted the Jews to spread His word to the world and "be a blessing to the world." The Temple should have been a prime vehicle to do this. Anyone should have been able to come to the Temple and encounter God and see Godly behavior from the people and priests in the Temple. *What kind of fruit was the Temple producing? What kind of fruit was the Temple leadership producing?* Read Mk 12:38-44 to see what they were doing. The Temple leadership used their positions to cheat and steal from the very people they were supposed to protect. Even worse, they had turned God's house into a livestock market and public thoroughfare. Was this good?

The Temple sat at the main Eastern gate into Jerusalem. Anyone entering town had a choice to make. They could take a short cut through the Eastern gate and through the middle of the Temple, or they could go around the walls of Jerusalem until they came to the Northern or Southern gate. Normally, this would be no problem. The people could ritually purify themselves by "baptizing" themselves in a Mikveh (immersing pool) and then respectfully make their way through the Temple.

The problem came when they had a herd of sheep, goats, camels or donkeys loaded with produce and also decided to go through the Temple. In effect, they treated the Temple and the presence of God as a short cut. Don't even start thinking about what a herd of animals always leaves behind.

In addition, the priests had a nice little monopoly business going on. You were required to produce a lamb without fault for them to use as a Passover sacrifice. You could bring your own lamb from home, but the priest had to certify that it was "faultless." If the priest found any blemish, the lamb could not be used. Since the priest had a large number of "pre-certified faultless" lambs for sale, the traveler seldom had a chance to use his own lamb.

The problem with buying a Temple lamb was that normal money couldn't be used in the Temple. The Passover pilgrim had to go to a moneychanger for the right money. The priest-approved moneychangers conveniently had their tables right next to the corrals of "pre-certified" lambs and were free to charge whatever they wanted to change the pilgrims' money into Temple-approved money. Anyone want to guess how much the moneychangers charged for this? Anyone want to guess how much of that the Priests got?

The bottom line was that the people used God's Temple as a short cut. God's priests used it as a stable and a way to use religion to cheat people out of their money. How would you feel if you came home and found this going on in your living room? No wonder Jesus was mad.

One last important detail. The fig tree was so closely associated with the nation of Israel and the Temple that they used fig leaves on coins to represent Israel. The Temple Holy of Holies building itself was decorated with fig leaves. Fig leaves, Israel, and the Temple were as closely connected to the Jews as baseball and apple pie are with America.

Now in the context of all this, how does Jesus' treatment of the fig tree fit into what happened in the Temple? What did Jesus expect to find when He went over to the fig tree? Did it look like it was healthy and able to produce fruit? Was it producing fruit? Why did Jesus say what He did about the fig tree? **Notice** *that He did not kill the fig tree, but made a prediction about its fruitfulness in the future. What kind of fruit was Jesus expecting to find in the Temple when He visited it? What happened to the Temple after Jesus died (Mk 15:38)? What do you think this means? Does it mean that God has left the building? How long did the Temple last after Jesus was crucified? If God was not in the Temple, was there any reason for the Temple (and the Temple leadership) to exist? (Hint: the Temple was destroyed about 35 years after Jesus was crucified, and yes, the Romans said that the Holy of Holies was empty when they went in.)*

Some people think the fig tree was an acted out parable that Jesus used to explain His actions in the Temple. What does this story have to say about the church today? What do you think?

MARK 11: *Jesus enters Jerusalem*

Mountain-Moving faith - Mk 11:22-26

Does Jesus always grant every request? Does God always grant every request? Are there any conditions on how and what we should ask God? Is it more important for us to ask God for things or for us to really listen to what God is asking us to do?

Again, this is one of those things I can't prove, but it is interesting. We normally associate moving mountains with God's power and our faith. In the context of Jerusalem, there was another option. As we said before, in order to have a flat space to build his Temple, Herod actually took the tops off two mountains and used the dirt to fill in the valley between the two mountaintops. In addition, Herod built his own mountain from scratch on a level plain in order to have a nice site for his palace and a protected place for his tomb. You can still see the Herodian mountain today from Jerusalem. I wonder if Jesus used either of these two "mountains" as an example. If so, it adds even more power to His point because there were two physical examples of mountains being moved. If a man, Herod, could do this, how much more could God do?

Herodian - The mountain that Herod built to contain his mausoleum

MARK 11: *Jesus enters Jerusalem*

The fortress that Herod built on top of his mountain in order to protect his mausoleum

Let the Confrontations Begin - Mk 11: 27-33

Mk 11:27-33 is a classic honor/shame confrontation. The leaders think they have Jesus trapped in a no-win situation. Jesus showed them that it was very hard to confound God. In an honor challenge, if you couldn't answer the challenge question acceptably, you were publicly shamed and you lost your honor status. In the challenge, it was acceptable to ask a counter question. If the person asked the question couldn't answer, he lost status and the ability to challenge you.

In this case, if the chief priests, scribes and elders answered Jesus' question, they automatically admitted that Jesus came from God. They lost either way, so Mark showed them slinking away – shamed. Jesus then proceeded to teach them – something you did to people who were ignorant and needed instruction. *How do you think the Pharisees felt about that? Even worse – the Pharisees understood exactly what Jesus said about them (Mk 12:12). Are we in danger of challenging Jesus' honor today? When we demand through prayer that He do what we want Him to do, are we making improper demands on Him?* Remember the man "telling" the disciples to cure his son? *Does that sound like us today?*

MARK 11: *Jesus enters Jerusalem*

ACTIVITIES

Create a narrative outline of the chapter, a list of the characters and a list of the titles used in the chapter.

Questions for further discussion or reflection

1. What are the three major events that happen in this chapter? How do these events fit into what Jesus has been saying about His time in Jerusalem? What is the significance of Jesus riding in on a donkey over palm fronds and people's clothes? Where does the quote in verse 9 come from? Read Ps 118:22-29. What is the significance of this quote? Who did the people think Jesus was?

2. What was the first thing Jesus did once he came to town? Where would you expect God's Son to go when He came to town?

3. How would you act if you were going to be within a few hundred feet of where God Himself "lived?" Would you dress up and make sure you were ritually clean? How would you feel if you entered the governor's mansion and criminals were running an identify theft ring and a meth lab in the lobby? Would it make you wonder about the governor and the government he represented? Would you be just a little aggravated about what they had done to your father's house?

4. Did Jesus steal the donkey? Why do you think He did or did not? Was there anything significant about the donkey? Read Mk 14:13-16 when Jesus again sent out His disciples. Do you see any similarity? How did Jesus know about the room and the donkey? Was it Divine knowledge or did He have some secret disciples in the city?

5. Why did Jesus say that He was cleaning the Temple? Remember this was His Father's house. What was going on in the Temple? Why was this bad? What was expected to go on in the Temple? What was one of God's first purposes in taking the Jews as His own people? What kind of fruit was the Temple leadership producing? Read Mk 12:38-44 to see what they were doing.

6. Are we in danger of challenging Jesus' honor today? When we demand through prayer that He do what we want Him to do, are we making improper demands on Him? Remember the man "telling" the disciples to cure his son? Does that sound like us today?

The Gospel of Mark

Mark 12: Jesus Indicts the Temple Leadership

- Herodians and Pharisees take their best shot
- The Sadducees try to rally the retreating troops
- A scribe finally asks a good question and gets a proper answer
- Activities: Questions for further reflection

MARK 12

Jesus Indicts the Temple Leadership

The confrontation starts in Mk 11:27, when the Temple leadership attacks Jesus. Jesus defeats them and tells a very pointed parable about them in order for everyone to understand exactly how bad the leadership has been. The point of the parable is that the owner of the vineyard gave some people temporary use of the resource.[37] The owner didn't sell the vineyard. He rented it to them. The rent would normally include some of the harvest as payment. The renters liked the situation so much, they got confused over who actually owned the resource. They thought they controlled the vineyard and went so far as to kill the owner's son so they could have uncontested ownership of the vineyard. There might be a modern day sermon here.

The religious leaders were confused over the purpose and ownership of the Temple. Because they controlled the physical building, they thought that they controlled access to God and perhaps even controlled God Himself. They were supposed to be producing a harvest for God and they were taking everything for themselves. Apparently this was so well known that the people listened to the parable and agreed with its point. In their opinion, Jesus' description of the Temple leadership was just about right.

In addition to the yearly Temple tax that every Jew in the entire world had to pay, the Temple made money through changing money and selling acceptable sacrifices. There was nothing wrong with either of these two things, but apparently the Temple used the money changing and sacrifice selling as a way to cheat people out of their money. Even worse, they used God's house as a site and an excuse to cheat people who were trying to worship God. The Temple had so much money, the rulers literally did not know what to do with it. This is not an exaggeration. When Jerusalem was destroyed in the 66-70 AD Jewish revolt, the Temple was plundered and the money in the Temple treasury was sent back to Rome. If you want to see one of the ways the money was used, look at the Coliseum in Rome.

---

[37] *Does this sound like Israel? Remember Israel is the land of grapes and wine (Num 13:23).*

Instead of using the money to take care of widows and orphans as the Law required, the Temple leadership used its authority and power as a way to take away the little bit the widows had (Mk 12:38-40). The point was that the Temple leadership had become such an obstacle to God that He was going to take them out of the way. The Temple leadership got the point and went off defeated, publicly shamed, but ultimately unconvinced (Mk 12:12). Of course, we never do the same thing today, do we? **First quarter score: Jesus 1 – Temple Leadership 0.**

The Herodians and Pharisees Take Their Best Shot

The Temple leadership was still trying to publicly shame Jesus so He would lose status and popularity with the crowd. Since the Temple leadership no longer had any status with the common people, they sent in a group that might be more popular with the crowd. In general, the Pharisees were completely opposed to the Temple leadership and were popular with the common folk who had flooded Jerusalem for Passover. The Herodians were Hellenized Jews who probably weren't popular with the crowds, but may have been along to protect the Temple's interests. This is the same strangely mismatched coalition that got together back in Mk 3:6 in order to plot Jesus' death.

The Temple leadership tried to trap Jesus in the famous game of three questions. Actually, I made up the idea of the game, but the concept of three testing questions was common among the Jews. It was similar to the types of questions deacons might ask someone going through his or her ordination. The questions were designed to cover a variety of theological, legal (Torah Law), and ethical topics. If the person could answer the questions correctly (in the opinion of the questioners), then he was considered acceptable. If the person couldn't answer the questions, then he was shamed and shunned. The difference is that the leadership weren't asking Jesus fair questions designed to demonstrate His knowledge even though the questions covered the standard theological, legal and ethical territory.

Notice that they started by building up Jesus' status, just so He would have farther to fall when He couldn't answer the question correctly. In fact, they created a question that they believed would trap Jesus.

The first question was impossible to answer without offending someone and failing someone's standards. If Jesus agreed about paying the poll-tax to Caesar that all Jews hated with a passion (remember that until Rome conquered them, they were in a tax-free situation), everyone

MARK 12: *Jesus indicts the Temple leadership*

would hate Jesus. If He spoke against the tax, the Romans would consider Him a rabble-rouser trying to steal money from Caesar and put Him in prison for tax evasion.

The key to Jesus' response was that it was absolutely forbidden for a Jew to have a coin with anyone's image on it. The image was considered a "graven image" and was specifically forbidden by Torah Law. (Remember this is a question about the Law.) Once the Jews demonstrated they had the coin with Caesar (god) on it, the testing was officially over. Jesus' answer no longer mattered. The very people who claimed authority to judge Jesus' compliance with the Torah Law demonstrated that they didn't follow the Law themselves. It was like they used their own false tax returns to accuse Jesus of filing false tax returns. The IRS is likely to say, "We will get to Jesus in a minute, but first, we have questions for you about your tax returns."

Even though the Pharisees and Herodians were already defeated, Jesus went on to answer their question in a way they hadn't anticipated. The money wasn't acceptable to any good Jew, so it might as well be used for a purpose that wasn't acceptable to any good Jew – support of the earthly Roman empire. Jesus went beyond the Law and expounded on the underlying theology. Ultimately, worldly things are only useful for worldly things. The true answer was that they should be focused on heavenly things of eternal importance. Yes, the crowd was amazed. **Second Quarter Score: Jesus 2 - Jews 0. (If this keeps up, Jesus may get a hat trick before the fight is over.)**

The Sadducees Try to Rally the Retreating Troops

Before we get started with this round of the contest, remember that the Sadducees didn't even believe in the resurrection. They didn't believe in the resurrection because they only considered the first five books of the Bible to be authoritative. If it wasn't in the Torah, they didn't believe in it. Since resurrection wasn't mentioned in the Torah, they didn't believe in resurrection. This throws their question into a whole new light, doesn't it?

This question sounds like one of those press conference questions where the reporter hates the person being interviewed and does his or her best to ask a convoluted question that no one could keep track of and then expects a lucid short answer from the poor person who has to respond to the question. The question is on the order of, "If God is all powerful, can He create a rock that weighs too much for Him to lift or, "Do you still beat your wife?" How do you answer a question like that?

Jesus accused the Sadducees of not knowing or understanding the Scriptures (a deadly insult) and then demonstrated His own understanding by using the Scriptures to instruct the Sadducees in the resurrection. *Did you notice what Scriptures Jesus quoted? Was it from one of the first five books of the Bible? Do you see how Jesus used the very Scriptures the Sadducees considered authoritative to prove their ignorance?*

Jesus again demonstrated His power to describe God's purpose. The whole point of the Leverite marriage (which is what the question was about), was a way to preserve the land inheritance of someone who died without children. The brother "married" the widow so the inheritance could stay in the family. Once everyone died, the concept of Leverite marriage no longer applied. No one needed anything other than God to assure his or her eternal inheritance. Our eternal inheritance comes not from whom we are married to, but directly from God (like the angels). **Third Quarter Score: Jesus 3 – Jews 0.** Is there no one left who can put this man in his place?

A Scribe Finally Asks a Traditional Question and Gets a Proper Answer

All of the trick questions have failed, so someone finally asks an appropriate question. The idea of greatest or first commandment was very popular in the first century and we have many rabbinical responses to the question. In general, they agree with Jesus. Jesus didn't stop there, but went on to give the scribe a little something extra with the second greatest commandment. On hearing Jesus' response, the scribe declared Jesus' answer correct and acceptable. Jesus was publicly judged and named a "right" or "good" teacher who could use the Scripture righteously. The scribe announced the final verdict of the inquisition about Jesus. In return, Jesus gave the scribe the status of someone who was close to the Kingdom of God. Notice the scribe is near, but not in the Kingdom of God. **Final Score: Jesus 4 – Jews 0.**

Mark ended the confrontation chapter with a bad example and a good example of the proper behavior in the Kingdom of God. The bad example was the scribes who cared so much for worldly money and things that their whole reward was what physical things they had and what worldly praise they received. Jesus contrasted that to the widow who had nothing but faith in God, which was worth more than all the rest.

Now get ready for a real shift. Jesus changed from defending Himself to giving His disciples some last-minute teaching in order to answer their questions.

MARK 12: *Jesus indicts the Temple leadership*

ACTIVITIES

Create a narrative outline of the chapter, a list of the characters and a list of the titles used in the chapter.

Questions for further discussion of reflection

1. Have you gotten into any confrontations about your faith? How did you handle the situation? Were you as patient as Jesus? Have you thought about what it might mean if you haven't gotten into a confrontation or at least a discussion about your faith recently? Will the world ever truly accept and be happy with a sincere Christian? Think about Paul before you answer that question.

2. What kind of resources have you received from God and how do you use those resources? Are you a better steward than the Temple priests? In the time of Jesus, the big question for the Jews was how to live with the Roman occupation. Did you accommodate and become more Roman than the Romans (Sadducees) or did you turn away and become a extremely strict follower of the law (Pharisees)? What kind of accommodations do we make with the world today? Are we really any better than the Pharisees or Sadducees? Notice that Jesus showed a different kingdom and a different way to be pleasing to God.

3. If you had the opportunity to ask Jesus one question, what would it be? How do you think He would answer it?

4. Why do you think Mark included the confrontation at this point in his Gospel? What point do you think he was trying to make? Keep that in mind as you go to the next chapter.

THE GOSPEL of MARK

Mark 13: The Pause Before the Passion · The "Little Apocalypse"

- Warning about the interpretation of Mark 13
- Context of the passage
- Grammar of the passage
- Abomination of Desolation
- The Apocalypse (end of the world)
- Final summary
- Activities: Questions for further reflection

MARK 13

The Pause Before the Passion - The "Little Apocalypse"

A message from the cockpit. Please return to your seats and make sure your seatbelts are securely fastened. There may be some turbulence ahead.

OK, here we go. Let me start off by saying that many well respected Christians and scholars believe this entire chapter is about the end of the world. Many people call this chapter the "Little Apocalypse" because they think it refers to the end of the world as explained in the book of Revelation. I may be completely wrong about what I am going to write, but I think it fits the text. You don't have to agree with me and I won't question your salvation if you disagree with me. Please don't question mine. I really want us to try and focus on what the text says as opposed to what we have heard that it says. Hey, that is almost Biblical, isn't it?

Context of the Passage

First of all, let's look at the context. Jesus has cleaned the Temple and used the parable of the fig tree to warn of the coming destruction of the Temple. The parable of the vineyard also warns the Temple rulers of an accounting. In Mk13:2, they are looking at the magnificence of the Temple and Jesus warns that the Temple will be destroyed (not one stone standing on top of another). Mk 14 deals with the Last Supper and the arrest and trial of Jesus. *This is the pause before the Passion. Why do you think Mark put this chapter were he did? What question did the disciples ask?*

Mark 13:4 (NASB) "Tell us, when will **these things** be, and what [will be] the sign when all **these things** are going to be fulfilled?"

Given the context of what is happening in the discussion between Jesus and the disciples, it makes more sense to think that "these things" are the destruction of the Temple in 68-70 AD and not necessarily the end of the world.

Mk 13:2 tells us they (the four disciples) were sitting on the Mount of Olives and talking to Jesus privately. From the Mount of Olives you can see down into Jerusalem and the Temple. The Mount of Olives also has great eschatological significance. (Eschatological is a theological buzzword to refer to the "end times.") When Jesus returns, He will first set foot on the Mount of Olives and then triumphantly enter Jerusalem through the East gate. *What do you think they meant by the phrase "these things" in Mk 13: 4? Were they asking Jesus about the end of the world, or were they continuing to ask Him what he meant about the Temple being destroyed?* So far, no one in Mark 13 has said anything about the end of the world. Don't get too worried; I think Jesus talks about the end of the world in this chapter, but just not in the first part of the chapter.

Grammar of the Passage

Now, let's look at some Greek grammar. Here is a list of the imperative verbs of command in the chapter. One group of imperatives is the command to "look," "watch," "be alert" and "understand or don't be deceived" in verses 5, 9, 14, 23, 28, 33 (twice), 35 and 37. Other imperatives are in verses 7 (don't be frightened), 11 (don't worry and say), 14 (flee), 15 (go down) and 21 (believe). I don't know if that is the record for the most imperatives in a single chapter, but it is a whole bunch of them. What do all these imperatives mean? Jesus wasn't giving advice. He was commanding His disciples. **Notice** what kind of commands He gave His disciples. *Do you think that might be the point of this passage?*

Once the four disciples have asked Jesus about "these things," what is Jesus' response in Mk 13:5? I think this is a big key to the meaning of the passage. Jesus' response is not to first tell them about what is going to happen, but to order (imperative) them to not let anyone deceive them. I think the chapter is a warning not to be deceived by false prophets and false signs of the end times or Temple destruction. I do think some of Mk 13 talks about the end of the world, but I think the main point is a warning against deceptive signs and false prophets for any time. Mk 13:23 repeats this message with another imperative not to be deceived. Jesus is telling them not to be deceived because He is warning them about it in advance.

One final bit of Greek geekness in Mk 13:5. One of the reasons I like Greek so much is that it is a very Southern language. "Y'all" is no longer considered proper English grammar, but y'all has always been a part of the Greek language (also Hebrew, but don't get me started). There is a specific pronoun the Greeks use for the plural form of "you." It perfectly fits the Southern use of y'all. Just to show you that Greek wasn't the last answer to language sophistication, the Greeks never developed the concept of "all y'all."

My point is that most English translations of Mk 13:5 end with the pronoun "you." What is written in Greek is the pronoun "y'all." Jesus is referring to something the four disciples need to be careful not to be confused about. Jesus is talking to them and warning them personally. Since I don't think the world has ended yet, Jesus can't be warning them about the end of the world. To save us all from a lot of Greek grammar, the y'alls continue until Mk 13:24. Until that verse, my interpretation of this is that Jesus was warning the disciples specifically about something they would be exposed to. This was a personal and not a general warning. I may be wrong about my interpretation, but my Greek grammar is correct.

What was Jesus warning them about? I think, deception (Mk 13:5), violence (Mk 13:7-8) and persecution (Mk 13:9) of any kind. In Mk 13:7 and Mk 13:8 Jesus reminded the four disciples that these things were merely signs of the beginning - they were not the end.

The Abomination of Desolation

What was the abomination of desolation? Some say it happened during the Jewish Civil war in 168 B.C. Some say it happened at various times during the Jewish rebellion and sack of Jerusalem in 70 AD. Some say it will happen at the end of time, when the Antichrist performs a sacrifice in the newly rebuilt Temple. I don't know what the right answer is. I do know that the text used the same verb form of "y'all" that had been used for the whole chapter. It appears to me that Jesus started talking to the disciples using the verb form "y'all." He continued with the same form in this verse. This makes me think that Jesus was referring to something that the disciples would see. I could be absolutely wrong about this. *What do you think? Read through the passage and put in y'all instead of you. Does it make a difference in how you interpret the passage?*

If this is the end of the world, what good does it do to flee to the mountains (Mk 13:14)? How do you interpret the additions and changes to this passage that Matthew and Luke make? Read Mt 24:15. Matthew helps us out a little bit by telling us that the abomination of desolation is what Daniel was talking about. This helps some, but is not definitive. It sounds like it involves something standing in the Holy of Holies, but that still could be several things. Luke finally gives us a clear answer in Lk 21:20. Now this I can understand. Thanks, Luke. Even I can see how to apply this. When the city is surrounded, don't be caught on the wrong side of the troops.

MARK 13: *The pause before the passion*

When Rome attacked Jerusalem, they built a wall around the entire city so no one could escape. If you waited until the troops were there, you were going to be trapped inside the wall. Once the wall was complete, the Romans killed everyone and destroyed everything inside the wall. Rome did not mess around with people who challenged her power.

During the Jewish revolt, Jews from all parts of the empire returned to Jerusalem to defend the city against the surrounding Roman army. They were all killed in the defeat and sack of Jerusalem. The reason they came back was to defend the presence of God (Holy of Holies in the Temple) from Roman desecration. They were willing to die to protect the holiness of God. *Is Jesus telling His disciples that it's not worth it to stay and die in Jerusalem in order to preserve the Temple?*

Go back and read Jesus' denunciation of the Temple and its leadership in Mk 11-12. Would Jesus want His disciples to die defending a withered fig tree? Pretty clearly to me, Jesus is telling them not to worry about Jerusalem. By that time, the Temple will no longer contain the presence of God. Remember this when we get to the tearing of the Temple veil in Mk 15. *Was that so people could get into the presence of God or was that evidence that the presence of God was leaving the Temple?*

The Apocalypse (end of the world)

Notice the verb shift in Mk 13:24-27. The first word "but" indicates a change in subject, and the "y'alls" change to "they." Is Jesus still talking to the disciples? Why did He shift His form of address? I believe that these verses refer to the end of time and Jesus is talking about "they," the people who will experience the end. Another way to tell the change in subject is the key phrase, "in those days." This is a characteristic phrase in the Old Testament to refer to the judgment day. Clearly Mk 13:26 referred to Jesus' return at the end of the world. But be careful. Mk 13:29 returns to y'all. The generation that will not pass away before these things happen is another y'all.

Mark 13:30 (NASB) "Truly I say to y'all (my translation), this generation will not pass away until all these things take place."

Jesus changed the subject and summarized His comments in the next few verses. One of the big challenges you have to decide for yourself is verse 30. What does "all these things" refer to? Does it include the coming of Jesus after the tribulation? Or does it refer to all the things outside of verses 24-27? Here are some options. Verses 24-27 were fulfilled during the crucifixion and ascension of Jesus and the other verses apply to the destruction of the Temple. "This generation" was generic and referred to everyone living in the end times (after the death of Jesus). If "this generation" was literal, how does that affect your interpretation? Keep in mind that so far as we know, Jesus has not yet returned. *Has Jesus given the disciples some personal advice about what to do when Jerusalem is surrounded, some advice about the true end of the world, and then returned to personal advice about what they need to do?*

Here is my paraphrase. Don't be misled by false prophets of doom. Since y'all are asking Me, here is how the Temple is going to be destroyed. I am telling y'all now so y'all won't be tempted to return and be killed in a senseless death. Now don't y'all be confused. The world will eventually end. The sun will go out and the moon will be darkened. "They" (an exact quote from Mk 13:26) will see Me coming in my glory. Until these things happen, don't y'all worry about the end of the world. Now keeping all of this in mind, let me summarize. Be alert, but y'all don't be confused. Only God knows when the world will end (**Notice** the phrase "that day" again). Anyone claiming differently is confused. Y'all be ready! (Jesus probably said it better.)

What does it mean that not even Jesus knows when the end will be? I thought He knew everything?

The word "alert" appears five times in the last four verses. What do you think this means? What point do you think Jesus was trying to make? You don't have to be a rocket scientist to figure this one out.

A Final Attempt at Summary (Have I said that I might be completely wrong?)

In Mk 13, Jesus tells the disciples not to be deceived. When Jerusalem falls, it might seem like the end of the world, but it isn't. Don't rush back to defend something that has lost its purpose and that God has decided needed to be destroyed. When the world really ends, everyone will know it. So be ready and alert, but don't be deceived.

MARK 13: *The pause before the passion*

ACTIVITIES

Create a narrative outline of the chapter, a list of the characters and a list of the titles used in the chapter.

Questions for further discussion or reflection

1. Why do you think Mark put this chapter were he did? What question did the disciples ask? How do you think Jesus answered His disciples? Does the overall context and specific location of the discussion help you understand what the chapter is about?

2. What do you think they meant by the phrase "these things" in Mk 13:4? Were they asking Jesus about the end of the world, or were they continuing to ask Him what He meant about the Temple being destroyed?

3. The word "alert" appears five times in the last four verses. What do you think this means? What point do you think Jesus was trying to make? You don't have to be a rocket scientist to figure this one out. 😎

4. What do you think the "Abomination of Desolation" referred to? Why do you think Matthew and Luke add detail to the description in this passage?

5. Not to start an argument about the end times, but does this chapter make you skeptical of people who predict exactly what events are leading up to the end of the world and claim to know the exact date? What do you think Jesus would say to them?

The Gospel of Mark

Mark 14: *The Passion Approaches*

- The anointing of Jesus
- Passover
- Garden of Gethsemane
- Devotion - Our Passover lamb in the Kidron Valley
- The trial of Jesus
- Peter's denial of Jesus
- Activities: Questions for further reflection

MARK 14

The Passion Approaches

Anointing, Arrest, and Trial

After a refreshing pause to talk about the end of things, Mark continues with what is known as his "Passion narrative." In my Bible, the Passion narrative takes up almost seven pages out of a total of 32 pages. This works out to 22% of the entire Gospel. Mk 14 is 3½ pages long. As the action slowed down, Mark started taking his time in describing things. Notice that he gave us more action and more detail. *Why do you think Mark spent more time with this section?* If you aren't still making a list of what happens in each chapter, do it for chapters 14-15. In Mk 14, you have the anointing of Jesus, Passover, Garden of Gethsemane, Arrest of Jesus, Trial of Jesus, and Denial of Jesus. It's a long chapter, but Mark was really packing it full of material. My point is that all of this must be very important to Mark and his audience. It is up to us to figure out what Mark was telling us and why he gave us so much detail.

Anointing of Jesus - Mk 14:1-11

Why was it a big deal for the woman to anoint Jesus with this perfume? Think about the status of women at this time. Were they normally invited to dinner? Where do you think this woman came from? What was she doing at dinner? Many people assume the woman is Mary Magdalene. Do they have any reason to believe this?

It is difficult to list how many social and cultural barriers are being crossed in this passage. Most first century dinners consisted only of close family or friends and women were not invited to eat with the men. Even if women were there, it would have been considered beyond the pale to let one of them interrupt dinner by anointing a guest's head with oil. Even if the situation could be considered appropriate in some cases, it was not the kind of thing you would do at the dinner table. First century Rabbis avoided any kind of contact with women who weren't close family members. Given how many barriers are being crossed, the fact

MARK 14: *The Passion approaches*

that the disciples only complain about money is very significant. *Why do you think they didn't complain about the other social mistakes that Jesus apparently made?*

Exact equivalents of cost are hard to determine, but in general, the perfume probably represented about a year's wages. It was an incredibly expensive and extravagant gift. Jesus puts it in perspective when he describes the anointing as preparation for His burial. Again we can't tell for sure, but the woman apparently gave Jesus a gift of the thing that was most precious to her. *Just for grins, does anyone see any parallels to the widow's mite passage in Mark? Doesn't she also give everything she has? What did Jesus say about her offering? What does that mean to us today?*

Notice how often the disciples were concerned about money. Go back and reread the feeding of the multitude stories. *Weren't they worried about money then? Do you remember Jesus ever getting worried about money? Was there one particular disciple at the table who apparently was very concerned about getting some money (Mk 14:11-12)?*[38] *When we read that the love of money is the root of evil, does it start making sense? Was Jesus any more worried about the cost of the perfume than He was about the cost of the bread? Was Jesus concerned back in Mk 4 when His disciples alerted Him to the life and death situation in the storm-tossed boat? Do we ever see Jesus worrying about anything?* We see Him struggling in the Garden of Gethsemane, but once His prayers are over, He seems to accept what is going to happen.

Passover - Mk 14:12-31

Verses 12-16 are very important because they make it plain that Jesus is getting ready to eat the Passover meal with His disciples. Passover represented the nation of Israel's delivery from oppression and slavery in Egypt and the creation of a new people and nation. It also represented deliverance from death. Remember that the angel of death "passed over" all the houses with lamb's blood painted over the door. There was a very specific ritual associated with how the Passover was eaten. There were set speeches and ceremonies all during the meal. Bread was offered in remembrance of the old covenant God made with the Jews. Wine was offered to remember that same covenant. Jesus is breaking the old ceremony here, with His new ceremony. Read Jer 31:31 and see if that gives you a clue about His new Covenant.

---

[38] *I really think you should pause and consider this. I think the principle is more than just not worrying. I think it probably starts with managing your expenses so you have less to worry about. Where do our money worries come from? In this life, we all need some money, but what is the minimum we really need?*

MARK 14: *The Passion approaches*

Notice that Jesus talks about a new Covenant. Think back to some of the Old Testament covenants God made with His people. *What kind of Covenant is Jesus making with His disciples and by extension with us? How will He seal this Covenant? If the symbolic tie-in with Passover is valid, what is He offering deliverance from? Or as Emma, my grammarian, would say, "From what is He offering deliverance?"* This ceremony became one of the earliest rituals of the new Christian church and is recorded in one of the earliest writings we have (1 Cor 23-26). Regardless of denomination, this is something all Christians are supposed to continue to do.

Garden of Gethsemane - Mk 14:32-52

Read the three different versions of what happens in the Garden of Gethsemane (Mt 26:36-46 and Lk 22:39-46). *What does Jesus warn the disciples about? What kind of temptation are they going to face? Do they prepare? Why did an angel appear to comfort Jesus (Lk 22:43)? What is the deal with sweating blood in Lk 22:44?* Notice that Jesus calls God, "Abba." This is a very personal form of address. I think this is the last temptation of Christ. Lk 4:13 says that after Satan failed at making Jesus sin in the wilderness, he (Satan) left Him (Jesus) until an opportune time. I think this is the opportune time. *Read Luke's Transfiguration story in Lk 9:31-32. What do you think Jesus, Elijah and Moses were talking about?*

Our Passover Lamb and the Kidron Valley

Looking down the Kidron Valley, Jerusalem and the Temple are to your right.

137

MARK 14: *The Passion approaches*

Looking up at the Mount of Olive from the Kidron Valley. Note the tombs covering the hillside. It probably looked very similar at the time of Jesus.

Looking up at the Eastern or Golden Gate in the Jerusalem city walls from the Kidron Valley. The Golden Gate is currently blocked, but I don't think that will stop Jesus when He returns.

MARK 14: *The Passion approaches*

Everybody knows the Gospel story about Jesus leaving Jerusalem on Passover and going to spend the night in the Garden of Gethsemane. Not everyone has thought about the details of that story and what they meant to Jesus and His disciples. *Why did Jesus and His disciples have a habit of spending the Passover nights in the Garden (Lk 22:39; Jn 18:1-2)? Was it a popular place for tourists? Why did they leave Jerusalem to find a place to sleep?*

The city of Jerusalem swelled with Passover tourists from a city of perhaps 60,000 to a city of 600,000+ people. There was not room for even a portion of the visitors to stay in the city, so each tribe or family had a traditional area where they stayed just outside the city. Some think that Jesus' family stayed close to the Mount of Olives within the traditional Sabbath day's journey from Jerusalem. This was far enough away to be able to find a place to sleep, but still close enough to get into Jerusalem for the Passover events. If Jerusalem was so full, why does it sound like the disciples were able to find privacy so near to Jerusalem, when there were so many people also trying to find a place close to Jerusalem? The Garden was probably private property and may have been fenced in, but there may be more to the story.

The Bible doesn't give us the answers, but we can make some educated guesses based on what we know about the geography and structure of Jerusalem. Here is what we do know. David crossed the Kidron Valley escaping from his rebellious son Absolom (2 Sam 15:23-30). King Asa burned the pagan idols and asherah poles (1 Kgs 15:13) in this valley. It was a major cemetery as far back as King Josiah (2 Kgs 23:6), and Jesus rode up the Kidron Valley on a donkey to enter the city of Jerusalem (Lk 19:28-44).

We see the Kidron Valley today as a busy thoroughfare, a green park, and massive cemetery. While the tombs were still there, it looked a lot different at the time of Passover in the first century. Jerusalem and the Temple had a real problem during Passover. Each family had to have their own Passover lamb sacrificed in the Temple. There were so many people that the priests couldn't kill the lambs quickly enough. They actually had to spread the Passover meal over two days in order to make sacrifices for all the people. We all know about eating the Passover lamb, but we forget about the preparation of more than 100,000 lambs.

As we stand at the bottom of the valley and look up at the walls of Jerusalem, we have to remember that water flows downhill. In addition to water, everything else also flows downhill. Blood had to be drained from each and every one of those 100,000+ Passover lambs and then the blood had to be disposed of. During the rest of the year, some of the blood was sold to local farmers as fertilizer, but at Passover, there was a lot left over. The Temple Mount was hollow and Herod built numerous massive cisterns under the Mount to hold the water required to clean the Temple of all the sacrificial blood. The blood was flushed out of the Temple and ran down through the Kidron Valley and eventually away from Jerusalem. While modern day archeologists have not been able to find the first century streambed, they know that it is there. After heavy rains today, there is a overflow creek that runs through the Kidron Valley.

While the Bible doesn't say, all of that blood coming down the middle of the Kidron Valley could not have smelled good or been pleasant to be around. This may be why people stayed up on the Mount of Olives and why the Garden was an unpopular place. Given the sanitation of the day and all the Passover blood, the floor of the Kidron Valley and the Garden were probably not pleasant places. Only the disadvantaged and those rejected from their traditional families' places would plan on staying in such a place.

Based on all this blood running down the middle of the valley, there are two theological points that I want to make. The first is that to get to the Garden, Jesus probably had to cross over or wade through that stream of Passover blood. As He was going to the Garden to pray, He had the stench of blood in his nostrils and was being vividly reminded of what was about to happen to Him. Our Passover Lamb was about to have His blood spilled in the same way that the Jewish Passover lambs were sacrificed. The Passover Lamb allowed the Angel of Death to pass over the houses that that spread the lamb's blood over their doors, ushered in their freedom, and foreshadowed the Old Covenant.

Our Passover Lamb delivers us from the Angel of Death, creates the New Covenant, and promises us eternity with God.

We rejoice in that eternal freedom, but here in the Kidron Valley, let us remember that our freedom was bought with the price of Jesus' blood. Where we are standing was probably once covered in the presence and stench of blood. Our blessing from God is not just something ethereal. It is real, present, and paid for in blood. Our God loved us enough to send His Son to be our Passover Lamb and be an eternal sacrifice for us.

The second point is that the Garden of Gethsemane is not the end of the story. Not even the resurrection or ascension is the end of the story. Jesus is coming back to His city one more time. We believe that His second coming will happen on the Mount of Olives. Jesus will make one more trip across the Kidron Valley and enter Jerusalem, but this time He won't be riding on a donkey. This time He will have all the heavenly and earthly trappings of power. He will move down the hill in a cloud of glory and majesty. Tradition has it that the enclosed Golden Gates in the city wall will be opened and Jesus will enter his City to usher in the new heaven on earth. Just as His sacrifice was real and physical, so will His return and celebration be real and physical.

Jesus' sacrifice is a blessing to us and a responsibility for us. Jesus told us that being His disciple meant being willing to take up a torture device and follow Him. Sometimes that following might mean wading through the Kidron Valley in order to get to the New Jerusalem. My prayer is that we are willing to follow God wherever He leads us.

Trial of Jesus - Mk 14: 53-65

Why do you think Mark spends so much time on the arrest and trial of Jesus? Are any charges against Jesus ever proven? Is Mk 14:62 a promise or a threat?

Why would Mark's audience care so much about the trial of Jesus? If Mark's audience were Roman, his readers would have been very familiar with trials and the Roman legal system. In Rome, criminal trials were a public spectator sport. With no Internet, Twitter, Facebook, or reality TV, the Romans had to get by on what they could watch in the public forums. NASCAR (I mean horse racing) was so popular that 300,000+ people would spend the weekend at the Circus Maximus in Rome watching the chariot races. Trial attendance was so popular that tickets were sold and people had their slaves stand in line to get good seats or a close standing spot.

Written accounts of trials were popular with those who could read, and the local pundits loved to tear apart trial speeches. Mark may have included the detail for the same reason Luke had so much detail about Paul's sea journey to Rome. People loved to hear the stories. In addition, Pilate declared Jesus as innocent (Mk 15:14) – very important if Mark was writing for a Roman audience. Mark also showed how the Jewish legal trial was a farce with the Jews turning Jesus over to Pilate for no other reason than envy (Mk 15:10). If someone in Mark's audience were thinking about becoming a Christian, this would have been a very important question for him to have answered.

There might be something deeper going on if you think about the persecution of Mark's Roman audience. *How would you approach Christianity if you were a pagan considering conversion?* Christianity was seen as a Jewish religion. If you were a seeker, you probably knew

MARK 14: *The Passion approaches*

something about Judaism and its roots. You would know that Judaism was centered on the Temple and that the High Priest was very important to everyday forgiveness and the annual atonement ceremony for all Jews, everywhere. You would also probably be interested in why the High Priest didn't seem to be a Christian or support Peter or Paul!

If Jesus really was the Son of God, why didn't He have the total support of the High Priest and Jews everywhere? Why would the leadership of the religion work so hard to kill Jesus? Was it worth the persecution you would face in becoming a Christian? How had other Christians faced similar or worse persecution? Did you have to be perfect in order to be a good disciple? Can you deny Jesus and still be a disciple? Are you starting to get one of the points of Mark's Gospel?

I think one of the things Mark had to do for his audience was to show them that Jesus did not receive a fair trial, that the High Priest acted illegally and immorally in convicting Jesus, and that Christianity was no longer centered in Jerusalem. The detailed trial scene may address all these concerns. The trial scene is as much an indictment of the Jewish Temple leadership as it is a defense of Jesus. Also **notice** that the Roman officials don't seem to have any problem with Jesus and go out of their way to try to preserve Him.

We see this same theme played out even more clearly in Acts with Peter and Paul (but I digress). Mark started explaining the conflict between Christ and the Jewish leadership as early as his second chapter, and a lot of the action in the Gospel showed that Jesus was the replacement for the Temple which no longer performed God's work (cursing of the fig tree). Now the conflict has come to the crisis point. Who appears to be right in this conflict?

Mk 14:62 may be a stronger claim to Jesus being God than you initially understand. It is perfectly natural to say, "I am" and then include something that answers the question about what I am. "I am tired. I am the living water." For those of us who are old enough "I am the walrus."[39] To say "I am" and then stop is completely unnatural. We are conditioned to want something to come after the "I am." For Jesus to just say "I am" is more than a little strange. John is even more clear in his "I am" sayings in his Gospel, but I think Mark has the same kind of thing going on. To explain, I have to bring in some more Greek.

---

[39] *Find someone old to ask about the "Paul is dead" controversy during the 1960s. They will know what you are asking about.*

MARK 14: *The Passion approaches*

In English, it takes two words to say, "I am." (Yes, I know that is pretty obvious. Hang in there with me, please.) In Greek, a verb can have the subject built into it so you only need one Greek word to say, "I am." The single Greek word for "I am" is *eimi*.[40] It literally means I am. Now way back in Ex 3:14 God introduces Himself to Moses by giving Moses His name. We all know that the Hebrew word for God, Yahweh, comes from this passage. Literally in the Hebrew the passage reads, "Yahweh asher Yahweh or I am who I am." God uses the "I am" twice without any direct object. God is the great "I Am."

Around 250 BC, so many Jews had stopped speaking and reading Hebrew and started speaking Greek that they could no longer read the Hebrew Bible. To address this problem, Hebrew scholars translated the Hebrew Bible into Greek and called it the Septuagint or LXX. It is valuable to us today because by reading it we can tell how people close to both the Hebrew and Greek languages translated concepts from Hebrew into Greek. In other words, it can tell us the closest Greek equivalent to the Old Testament Hebrew word.

OK, test time. *Does anyone remember what the Greek word for I am is? Does anyone want to guess how the Hebrew scholars translated God's name in Ex 3:14? Does anyone want to guess the significance of Jesus saying "eimi" without anything else? Is Jesus claiming Yahweh's name for Himself?* If you have any doubt, read Mk 14:63-64. The high priest heard this as a claim to be God and thought the blasphemy was worthy of the death penalty.

Now, to really go out on a limb. If Jesus were addressing Jews, He was probably speaking everyone's birth language, which was Aramaic or Hebrew.[41] Does anyone remember how to say "I am" in Hebrew (or Aramaic)? I don't know that Jesus stood in front of His accusers and said, "Yahweh," but I like to think that He did. It may explain why the religious leaders got so mad, so quickly. If Jesus were lying, He was guilty of blasphemy and subject to the death penalty. If Jesus were telling the truth, the religious leaders' lives should be overturned. Either way, Jesus was a severe threat to the established religious leadership.

---

[40] The Greek word sounds like the woman's name Amy, with the accent on the second syllable.

[41] In the first century, Hebrew and Aramaic were very similar.

MARK 14: *The Passion approaches*

Peter's Denial - Mk 14: 66-72

Does Peter succumb to temptation? Is what Peter did any different than what Judas did? How did the two men treat their sin? What significance is it that Peter was afraid even to admit to a slave girl that he knew Christ? Luke, as usual, added a detail. Read Lk 22:61. In Luke, Jesus looked at Peter when he denied Him for the third time. Can you imagine how Peter felt when he realized what he had done? Remember that Mark used Peter as a representative or spokesman for all of the disciples. I think the point here is that all the disciples deserted Jesus, not just Peter.

I believe the overall point is that you can fail as a disciple and still be a good Christian. I believe the difference between Peter and Judas was that Peter asked for and received forgiveness and Judas didn't. Would this have a meaning for Mark's Roman audience? Remember, they would know what happened to Peter in the 30+ years since Jesus' crucifixion. If church tradition is correct, Peter would have been in Rome close to the time Mark's Gospel was written.

Read the Christmas story. I always connect the crucifixion to the birth of Christ and Easter. You need to remember all three of them together. Jesus' birth represents emptying Himself and becoming human. His crucifixion represents His ultimate obedience and sacrifice for us, which allows us to approach God as His forgiven children. Easter reminds us that God keeps His promises and that death has been conquered. Jesus attained His glory by faithful obedience in the face of humiliation, persecution, pain and suffering. God may call us to do the same one day. Our example and promise of ultimate reward is Jesus. When we read of Jesus on the cross, remember that His crucifixion is His victory and our victory. The proof is the resurrection.

MARK 14: *The Passion approaches*

ACTIVITIES

Create a narrative outline of the chapter, a list of the characters and a list of the titles used in the chapter.

Questions for further discussion or reflection

1. Why was it a big deal for the woman to anoint Jesus with this perfume? Think about the status of women at this time. Were they normally invited to dinner? Where do you think this woman came from? What was she doing at dinner? Many people assume the woman is Mary Magdalene. Do they have any reason to believe this?

2. Does anyone see any parallels to the widow's mite passage in Mark? Doesn't she also give everything she has? What did Jesus say about her offering? What does that mean to us today?

3. Notice how often the disciples were concerned about money. Go back and reread the feeding of the multitude stories. Weren't they worried about money then? Do you remember Jesus ever getting worried about money? Was there one particular disciple at the table who apparently was very concerned about getting some money (Mk 14:11-12)? When we read that the love of money is the root of evil, does it start making sense? Was Jesus any more worried about the cost of the perfume than He was about the cost of the bread? Was Jesus concerned back in Mark 4 when His disciples alerted him to the life and death situation in the storm tossed boat? Do we ever see Jesus worrying about anything?

4. Read the three different versions of what happens in the Garden of Gethsemane (Mt 26:36-46, Lk 22:39-46 and Mk 14:32-52). What does Jesus warn the disciples about? What kind of temptation are they going to face? Do they prepare? Why did an angel appear to comfort Jesus (Lk 22:43)? What is the deal with sweating blood in Lk 22:44? Notice that Jesus calls God, "Abba."

MARK 14: *The Passion approaches*

5. Why do you think Mark spends so much time on the arrest and trial of Jesus? Are any charges against Jesus ever proven? Is Mk 14:62 a promise or a threat? Why would Mark's audience care so much about the trial of Jesus?

6. If Jesus really was the Son of God, why didn't He have the total support of the High Priest and Jews everywhere? Why would the leadership of the religion work so hard to kill Jesus? Was it worth the persecution you would face in becoming a Christian? How had other Christians faced similar or worse persecution? Did you have to be perfect in order to be a good disciple? Can you deny Jesus and still be a disciple? Are you starting to get one of the points of Mark's Gospel?

The Gospel of Mark

Mark 15: *The Earthly Humiliation and Heavenly Glorification of Jesus*

- The events
- Trial before Pilate
- Jesus' last words on the cross
- God's first response to Jesus' sacrifice - the Temple veil
- Activities: Questions for further reflection

MARK 15

The Earthly Humiliation and Heavenly Glorification of Jesus

We have finally come to the heart of darkness. This is the ultimate humiliation of Jesus, which God turns into the glorification of Jesus. What will Mark do with this? I ask that question because Mark has a real challenge. He has to wind up his Gospel and explain the theological significance of THE critical event in Jesus' life without resorting to a theological essay or long discussion. Somehow Mark needs to take the events that happened and have us understand the theological importance of those events.

Mark does this by reporting on events and then showing us various responses to those events. The meaning is in the events and explanation is in the response. Look at Mark's structure in Mk 15.[42]

1.	The Event	Trial before Pilate	15:1-15
	The Response	The soldiers mock Jesus	15:16-20
2.	The Event	The crucifixion of Jesus	15:21-27
	The Response	The bystanders mock Jesus	15:29-32
3.	The Event	The death of Jesus	15:33-38
	The Response	The centurion confesses Jesus	15:39

The first two responses are mocking – in line with the humiliation of Jesus. The third response is the climax of the Gospel, with the correct recognition of Jesus from the most unlikely source. Also notice that all the mockery about Jesus is ironically correct. People are speaking the truth in their ignorance. Mark tells us who Jesus is and why this is happening by narrating the events of the trial and crucifixion. Mark used the events of Jesus' encounter with Roman justice to warn his audience that it needed to be prepared to face the same sort of persecution, trial, and punishment.

---

[42] R. Alan Culpepper, *Mark: Smyth and Helwys Bible Commentary*. (Macon, GA: 2007), 537.

Just as Jesus warned the disciples in the Garden of Gethsemane to prepare them to resist the temptation to deny Jesus, the crucifixion warns Christians of what they must be ready to endure. If Mark was written in the late 50s or early 60s AD, Nero's crucifixion and persecution of Christians would have fulfilled the warning. Each event in the chapter is significant and deserves analysis. We will only have time to look at a few of them.

Trial Before Pilate – Mk 15:1-15

Pilate had a long and turbulent history with the Jews. He never got along with them and the Jews were eventually responsible for Pilate being called back to Rome and being fired. Pilate's relationship with the Jews was such that if they had suggested it was Thursday, Pilate would have been more than happy to pass a law saying that Wednesday was going to last for 48 hours and that Thursday would be skipped that week. If the Jewish leadership wanted Jesus killed, Pilate's first response would probably have been, "I don't care if he is guilty or not. If you want him dead, I want him preserved."

Mark doesn't include the full trial dialogue and we don't get the real reason Pilate finally went along with the Jews until we read Jn 19:12-13, where the Jews tell Pilate that if he doesn't kill Jesus, he won't be a friend of Caesar. The "friend of Caesar" name was code for being a proper and patriotic Roman. If you were a friend of Caesar, you could get away with almost anything. If you weren't a friend, you were an enemy of the Roman Empire. If the Jews could make a name like this stick, they could at least get him fired and perhaps even executed.

Again, note the power of names and titles. Pilate's political mentor in Rome had just lost his job and been executed by Caesar because he was charged and convicted of "not being a friend of Caesar." The Jewish leadership was in constant contact with Rome and could easily bring the same charge against Pilate. In fact, Pilate was eventually fired and returned to Rome based on Jewish leadership complaints to Caesar. Can you see how Pilate couldn't run the risk of being convicted of the same charge as his boss?

Jesus' Last Words on the Cross – Mk 15:34

Theological blood has been spilled about what Jesus' quote in Mark 15:34 really means. Some sincere Christian scholars say that Jesus' quote indicates that as Jesus became sin for us on the cross, God actually separated Himself from Jesus. Jesus' cry was based on the anguish He felt as God departed from Him. While this may be true theologically, I don't think that is really what the quotation meant. Don't get me wrong. I affirm the atonement of Jesus by His death. I just don't think that Jesus used the quote to indicate God's abandonment at that point. As always, I might be wrong and you don't have to agree with me.

Chapter and verse divisions in the Bible are relative new comers to the text. In the time of Jesus, they didn't even use books for their Bibles. They used scrolls, which made finding a text even harder. Can you imagine telling someone in the first century how to get to Jn 3:16? "Well, you unroll the scroll about 3 cubits and look for a mark that will show you where to begin reading." Many of the early scrolls actually had such "lectionary notes" added to the text, so the priest could tell where to start and stop reading the appropriate text for that day. One of the reasons early Christians moved to the book or "Bible" format was that it took up less space and was easier to reference and combine various letters or Gospels into one volume. (Now you know where we got the word "Bible," but I digress again.)

The way people referenced a Scripture passage was to quote the first line of the Scripture. Educated people knew the Old Testament well enough that the first line was all they needed to bring the entire passage to their mind. The Psalms in particular were very popular and well known, if for no other reason than people sang them all the time. Think about how Paul quoted the Scripture. He would say, "As it has been written," and then go on to quote a part of a passage. We often don't take the effort in our Bible study today, but if you go back and look at the entire passage of what Paul was quoting and the context of that passage, you will get a whole deeper understanding of what Paul was trying to convey. Paul never said, "Let's turn to Isaiah 53:1-12 where Isaiah talked about how Jesus was going to be the suffering servant who would redeem all of Israel." He assumed his readers knew the passage well enough to pick up on the meaning. In the same way today, if I say, "The Lord is my shepherd," most of you would automatically quote the rest of the first line of Psalm 23 and think about the context of the entire Psalm.

If you want to do an interesting study, read Is 53 and look at all the New Testament references in the margin. Then go to the New Testament texts and see how they used the Old Testament. Many times the New Testament usage is not even a direct quote, but only a reference. If you study the Bible, there is more to the New Testament's use of the Old Testament than we are accustomed to thinking about. Ever wonder why Isaiah is Paul's, and I think Jesus', second favorite "Scripture" to quote from? Just so you know, the Psalms were their favorite.

In the context of Mark, if I wrote about Jesus' trial and said, "You know the passage where Mark wrote, 'They took Him away and delivered Him to Pilate.'" You wouldn't necessarily need to know that was from Mk 15:1 and you would immediately think about the whole context of Jesus' trial before the Jews and Romans.

OK, given all that, what does Jesus' cry from the cross mean? Everyone agrees that Jesus is quoting Ps 22:1. Does the full context of Ps 22 give us any additional meaning to Jesus' words? (As a complete aside and truly not meant to be sacrilegious, how much of an impact would it have had if Jesus cried out from the cross, "Ps 22:1!" instead of quoting the passage?)

Ps 22 has several things that have an impact on its interpretation. The first is that the references in Ps 22 to piercing His hands and feet and casting lots for His clothes are clearly connected to Jesus' crucifixion. The Psalm is a prophetic commentary on the crucifixion. If it describes the events, it may also have something to say about the meaning of those events.

The second is that the Psalm is one of the lament Psalms. These Psalms often follow a pattern of asking God to fulfill His covenant obligations to protect and deliver His people. The standard format was to call on God while reminding Him how you had been faithful to Him, and then to remind God that when people do evil things to a faithful covenant follower and God doesn't do anything about it, it reflects poorly on the honor of God. Ps 22:1-8 does exactly this. Then the lament normally goes on to describe how poorly the faithful covenant follower is being treated (Ps 22:9-18) and calls on God to make everything right. The normal lament Psalm then ends in praise anticipating God's redemption and promising eternal praise for God. In other words, the Psalmist knew that God would fulfill His covenant and rescue His people even if He didn't immediately respond (Ps 22:19-31).

If the entire Psalm is a reminder to God that the person has been faithful and a call to God to rescue His follower, what impact does that have on the fact that Jesus used it from the cross? Does this make sense given Jesus' situation on the cross? Does the context of the Psalm help you understand why perhaps Jesus quoted from the Psalm? One last bit of supposition. John has Jesus crying out, "It is finished" as His last words from the cross (Jn 19:30). I checked with a real live, internationally known Hebrew scholar and he confirmed that the last words of Ps 22 can be translated as, "It is finished."[43]

---

[43] Dr. Dennis Cole, Professor of Old Testament and Archaeology occupying the Mcfarland Chair of Archaeology and Co-Director, Center for Archaeological Research at New Orleans Baptist Theological Seminary. Based on a conversation on December 2003.

While I can't prove it, I will always wonder if Jesus quoted the first few words and the last few words of Ps 22 from the cross.

God's First Response to Jesus' Sacrifice: The Temple Veil – Mk 15:37-39

The normal interpretation of the tearing of the Temple veil implies that in tearing the veil, God destroyed any barriers between Himself and mankind. Because of the death of Jesus, everyone had direct access to the Holy of Holies through the person of Jesus. Theologically, I again have no problem with this interpretation, but there may be more going on in the passage. One of my favorite professors from seminary, Dr. Bill Warren, had a unique talent of asking the question that totally transformed your thinking about a Biblical passage. He asked, "What if instead of letting people into the Holy of Holies, God tore the veil on His way out of the Holy of Holies?" If so, the Temple was truly empty after the crucifixion.[44] Something similar seems to happen in Ez 10-11 where God appears to leave the Temple and the city of Jerusalem.

One of the consistent themes in Mark is Jesus replacing the corrupt Temple. If God really left the Temple, it was the final indictment against a corrupt people using God's house to rob and cheat the people they were supposed to protect. What better way to indicate that God has indeed left the Temple than by tearing the veil and showing everyone that the presence of God was no longer in the Temple. Clearly there was no longer any purpose for the Temple or the corrupt leadership which supported the Temple. With the atoning death of Jesus, there was no longer any use for the old sacrificial system. Jesus' better sacrifice was a new and living way to stay in a relationship with God.

I don't know that we need to choose between the interpretations. Both may be correct and good. I do think it's interesting to think about God showing everyone that He refused to stay among people who used His name to reject and kill His Son.

---

[44] *When Rome sacked the Temple in 70AD, they entered the Holy of Holies and claimed that it was empty.*

MARK 15: *The earthly humiliation and heavenly glorification of Jesus*

ACTIVITIES

Create a narrative outline of the chapter, a list of the characters and a list of the titles used in the chapter.

Questions for further discussion or reflection

1. What does Jesus' cry from the cross mean? Everyone agrees that Jesus is quoting Ps 22:1. Does the full context of Ps 22 give us any additional meaning to Jesus' words?

2. If the entire Psalm is a reminder to God that the person has been faithful and a call to God to rescue His follower, what impact does that have on the fact that Jesus used it from the cross? Does this make sense given Jesus' situation on the cross? Does the context of the Psalm help you understand why perhaps Jesus quoted from the Psalm?

3. If you were a Roman citizen, would you have a better understanding of the hypocrisy of the Jewish leadership after reading Mk 15? Would the fact that a Roman governor had no problem with Jesus and considered Him innocent of the charges help you make up your mind?

4. Make a list of all the ways Jesus was mocked and then see if you can show how they were true statements. How do we handle mockers of Jesus today? Have we ever mocked Jesus ourselves? If He is our King, why aren't we more successful at obeying Him?

5. What do you think is the significance of a Roman officer recognizing Jesus as truly the Son of God. Remember that the centurion worked for god (Caesar).

Conclusion

Thank you for taking your time to read through Mark's Gospel with me. I know you could have chosen to travel through Mark with many different people and I appreciate you picking me. In preparation for our descent to the real world, return your imagination to normal, fold up your ability to ask questions, and get ready to check your phone for messages as soon as we touch down.

I pray that you have learned something from all the questions and at least one of them has had an impact on your daily life. I hope you discovered at least one new thing about who Jesus really is and how the culture He lived in helps us understand Him better. From my perspective, taking the time to read the Bible slowly and encounter the text like its original readers is a life changing experience. If you still have questions or have new questions, congratulations. You are now officially a student of the Bible. You might be ready to Join Emma, myself, Bart and others as we follow Jesus "On The Way."

As a final note, if you ever get the chance to go to Israel with a good tour group, make sure you go. I know there are questions about the cost, safety and even value of the trip. After all, everything took place at least 2000 years ago and a true spiritual experience can't happen in such a touristy environment can it? I am living proof that Israel is very safe and that the trip will change the way you read and understand the Bible. Even more, you will have an opportunity to encounter God in a way that you just can't in the United States. You have a real opportunity to come back from your pilgrimage a changed person who has a better relationship with God. If you don't believe me, talk to almost anyone who has made the trip and see what he or she says.

Since we are talking about Israel and it's Friday afternoon as I finish this conclusion, I will share with you what is a greeting as well as farewell in Israel, "Shabbat Shalom Y'all!"[45]

---

[45] *If we want to keep up the Jewish traditions, we would leave each other with the hope and blessing, "Next year in Jerusalem."*

www.ingramcontent.com/pod-product-compliance
Lightning Source LLC
Chambersburg PA
CBHW061253230426
43665CB00026B/2918